EVA SLONIM (née Weiss) was born in Bratislava, Slovakia, in 1931. A survivor of the Holocaust, Eva relocated with her family to Melbourne in 1948. She married Ben Slonim in 1953, and together they had five children, and many grandchildren and great-grandchildren, fulfilling Eva's wish to rebuild what was lost in Europe. A gifted storyteller, and deeply passionate about the importance of education and community, Eva has for many years given public talks on her experiences during the war.

Gazing at the Stars

MEMORIES OF A CHILD SURVIVOR

Eva Slonim

Black Inc.

Published by Black Inc.,
an imprint of Schwartz Publishing Pty Ltd
37–39 Langridge Street
Collingwood VIC 3066, Australia
email: enquiries@blackincbooks.com
www.blackincbooks.com

Copyright © Eva Slonim 2014
Eva Slonim asserts her right to be known as the author of this work.

ALL RIGHTS RESERVED.
No part of this publication may be reproduced, stored in a retrieval system, or transmitted in any form by any means electronic, mechanical, photocopying, recording or otherwise without the prior consent of the publishers.

National Library of Australia Cataloguing-in-Publication entry:

    Slonim, Eva, author.
    Gazing at the stars : memories of a child survivor / Eva Slonim.
    9781863956536 (hardback)
    9781863956543 (paperback)
    9781922231475 (ebook)
    Slonim, Eva.
    Jewish children—Slovakia—Biography.
    Jewish children in the Holocaust—Slovakia—Biography.
    Auschwitz (Concentration camp)—Biography. Holocaust, Jewish (1939–1945)—Personal narratives.
    Holocaust survivors—Biography. World War, 1939–1945—Personal narratives, Jewish.
    940.5318092

Cover design by Peter Long.

*In everlasting memory
of my beloved son Malcolm*

Foreword

One thing I remember learning at school is that there is no word in ancient Hebrew for 'history'. In its place is the word *zikaron*. I'm not sure why this piece of information has stuck with me over the years, but it has. I remember my teacher explaining that the literal translation of *zikaron* is 'memory', but that something is lacking in this translation. 'There is something about the word's meaning that just cannot be conveyed in the English language,' she said.

Perhaps this is because history and memory are indistinguishable in Judaism. The Jewish past is not understood as a series of events arranged in chronological order, but as a continuous tradition. To be part of Jewish history is to practise the Jewish tradition, and to find meaning in that tradition is to become part of a shared memory. *Zikaron* is not just the recollection of past experiences; it is also the communal memory of an entire way of life.

I was reminded of this word when I started working with Eva Slonim on her memoirs. Every Tuesday, for around four months, we would sit together in her study and talk about her past. I was amazed by the facility of Eva's memory; I often had to remind myself that she was only twelve or thirteen years old when most of these events took place. I was in awe of her ability to remain focused and composed while talking about moments of unimaginable suffering, of complete horror. She told me her story with perfect stoicism, almost as if it were someone else's.

I recorded all our conversations; listening back to them, as I later did, was more gut-wrenching than the conversations themselves. When I was not in Eva's warm and reassuring presence, I found the evil she encountered as a child overwhelming and incomprehensible.

It was when I started transcribing our conversations that I really heard the voice of the young Eva. I was seeing and experiencing history through a child's eyes. There has been such a huge emphasis on systematically archiving what happened during the Holocaust. This is of course necessary, but sometimes it can make history look like cold, hard facts, and the sounds of individual suffering can be swallowed up.

Eva and I spoke at length about why she wanted to write this book. One theme we continuously came back to was testimony. Eva is driven by a sense of responsibility to tell future generations about what happened to her and her family. She wants to teach her grandchildren about Jewish life before the Holocaust, to ennoble the idea of Jewish continuity, and to teach and warn the world at large about humanity's potential for evil.

I once suggested to Eva that another function of testimony is more personal. It allows individuals the opportunity to reflect on what has happened to them. It may offer catharsis or a sense of release, perhaps even a new perspective from which to interpret their past experiences.

Eva shook her head. 'No,' she said. 'There is no meaning in these memories. Reliving these memories is only difficult. I'm doing it for the next generation.'

When you read this book, then, you will hear two voices. One is Eva as we know her now, a historian speaking with the caution and guardedness of someone who has built an internal wall against extraordinary suffering. The other is the Eva who experienced this trauma for the first time, the one who remembers, the girl who first interpreted her experiences with the naivety and innocence of childhood.

In Eva's testimony history and memory are entwined in one expression. It is almost impossible now to interpret anything meaningful from what happened to Eva. The Holocaust still looms as a break from tradition, a fracture in Jewish history – in Eva's words, 'the final goodbye to an entire way of life'.

These memoirs are, first and foremost, an exercise of incredible courage. I believe this courage comes from Eva's knowledge that her story will be recorded. She writes for *zikaron*, the hope that, sometime in the future, her testimony – along with those of her peers – will become part of the Jewish tradition, told over and over, lived over and over. This record of a personal memory will become part of the shared memory of the Jewish people.

Oscar Schwartz

Readers will find a glossary of the foreign-language terms used in this book on pages 178–180.

Childhood

Palisády Ulica, Bratislava, early 1930s

In spite of everything, I remember Bratislava as a beautiful city. The Danube flows through it majestically. I remember how, on sunny days, we would cross the river by boat, or by bridge, and go to the parkland on the other side for picnics.

I was born in Bratislava on 29 August 1931, the second child of Eugene and Margaret Weiss. Their first child, Kurti, was their only son, my only brother. He was one year older than me, the only boy in our budding family. After me, my mother would give birth to another eight girls – Noemi, Marta, Esther, Judith, Renata, Ruth, Rosanna and Hannah – all born in almost yearly succession.

We lived in a grand three-storey apartment building. It stood tall and imposing opposite the president's palace. I remember it well: number sixty, Palisády Ulica.

My Papa bought Palisády 60 before he married my Mutti, Margaret Kerpel. I believe that their marriage was arranged, and that their wedding was held in Mattersburg, Austria – Mutti's birthplace – in 1929. Papa would have been twenty-six when they got married, and Mutti was two years younger.

Young men weren't supposed to get married until they had the means to provide for a family. Before Papa got married, he matriculated and started a successful textiles business. Papa would work all day and then travel at night to the various places that his business would take him, while studying accountancy and textile engineering part-time. He was enterprising, and tireless in his efforts to pass on this work ethic to his children.

During summer we would go for holidays in the Tatra Mountains, staying at a Jewish resort in Ľubochňa. It was an elegant place, and kosher. Fresh rolls were baked every day. Tall trees and mountains surrounded the hotel. Papa would always arrive late for our holidays; there was always some outstanding business matter that had to be attended to.

We girls used to race down the hillside, rolling all the way to the bottom. Noemi and I would compete to see who could eat more bread rolls. Papa used to watch us and pay us one crown for every roll we ate. Kurti was a reserved young boy and preferred to read on his own. Our younger sister Marta was a cute little girl with a fiery disposition. I remember an adult once said to her, 'You are so sweet I could eat you up,' and she replied, 'Gobble up your own children!' In Ľubochňa there was also a swimming pool, and we little ones were permitted to swim even though there was mixed swimming.

Papa's father, Solomon Weiss, came from Trnava in Slovakia. It was a small town. His wife, Ruzena Loewenrosen, was born in Yugoslavia. The year after my parents married, Solomon and Ruzena moved to Bratislava and joined them at Palisády 60. Pres Opapa and Pres Omama, as we called them, lived on the mezzanine floor. You would come through off the street, open the big wooden doors of our apartment building, climb up ten or so steps, and there was their place.

We all treated Pres Opapa and Pres Omama with great respect, especially Papa. At Papa's textile shop, his father sat in an elevated chair manning the cash register, commanding authority. He was tall and immaculate, sporting a small beard, a hat and a black suit. In some ways, Pres Omama receded into her husband's shadow. She mostly dressed in floor-length black gowns, beautiful lace-up short boots, black gloves and a large black hat. She would wear that outfit everywhere, even to the market.

Papa would visit his parents twice daily, and on *shabbat* he recited *kiddush* at their home before coming upstairs to make *kiddush* for his own family. He adored his parents.

My father's older brother, David, and his wife, Frida, lived on the second floor of Palisády 60 with their four children, Gabriel (whom we called Bobo), Ernst, Miriam and Ruti. Frida was from the Haber family, who lived in Nitra. Her beauty was known from Nitra to Bratislava.

Every *shabbat* we would gather to eat *seudah shlishit* with Pres Omama and Pres Opapa in their apartment. The men would sit on one side of the table, opposite the women and children, but I don't ever remember being told that's how we had to sit. That's just how it happened. We women liked to sit together and schmooze. I liked to talk to my cousin Miriam and my sister Noemi best. I sat between the two of them, and we chattered away about clothes and dress-ups.

We all lived together in the grand old building at Palisády 60. We were very close. It was not common for a family to all live together, as we did, but Papa's devotion to his family bound us as a remarkably tight unit.

Weiss & Kerpel

Palisády Ulica, Bratislava, 1930s

Papa and Uncle David were partners in the textile business. Their company was called Bratia Bruder Weiss, and the offices and shops were at 12–14 Michalská Brána, in the heart of the city.

The shop had two large display windows looking out to the street. Walking past, you could always see Pres Opapa sitting proud in his high chair and manning the cash machine, two shelves packed with goods behind him. On the second floor was an office and plenty of spare rolls of poplin and damask fabric, which was our shop's specialty.

Most of our customers were peasants who made a living through embroidery. David was more patient with the retail customers than Papa, so it was up to him to attend to their needs, whilst my father usually worked upstairs in the office, occupying himself with purchasing, manufacturing and wholesaling. When Papa thought someone was a procrastinator, he would just walk away from them or pass them on to Uncle David to deal with.

Papa and David had a younger brother who did not work but immersed himself in Jewish learning full-time at a *kollel* in the city of Dunajská Streda. His name was Uncle Shamu, and he lived there with his wife, Dena, and their four children, Ephraim, Gitl, Moshe and Yitl, all under the age of six. Shamu had a long beard, always wore his *tzitzit* visibly and presented himself as a strictly Orthodox Jew. None of the men in the *kollel* worked, so their livelihood became their wives' responsibility.

Papa opened a retail outlet for Uncle Shamu in Dunajská Streda, and Dena managed the shop. Papa provided them with merchandise free of charge, and they lived off the proceeds of the sales. Papa and David would never have considered studying instead of working. Still, they supported Uncle Shamu without question.

Uncle Shamu and his family would travel to Bratislava for the big Jewish festivals. Of them all, I liked *Pesach*, or Passover, best. I looked forward to being with my family and to having time off from school, but most of all I looked forward to getting new clothes.

I loved being with my cousins and sisters, dressed in our new *yom tov* garb, exquisitely groomed with ribbons in our hair, socks adorned with lace. A dressmaker would come to our home two or three weeks before *Pesach* to make all the clothing. We bought nothing off the rack. We even had embroidered collars on our nightshirts.

Mutti once arranged for us to learn how to sew and mend our own clothes. I found the idea of learning how to sew and stitch very boring. During our first lesson, I cut a big hole in my fabric on purpose, and I was excused from all further lessons.

My favourite outfit was a dress of light-blue organza in the empire style, with matching satin ribbons across the bust, finishing with a large bow on the sides hanging the length of the dress. I wore it with white patent-leather shoes. The dress was itchy, I remember, but I was prepared to put up with the discomfort because it was so beautiful.

We would sit around the table, which was always filled with typical Jewish food that Mutti and Frida had prepared – *kneidel* and chicken soup, boiled fish with nuts, huge roasted geese and goose liver, *tzimmes* (we had never heard of gefilte fish) – and we would sing songs. Pres Opapa used to sing a song about how much better it was to be a man than a woman. Mutti hated it; she always made him stop singing it.

*

Mutti was a quiet woman of strong conviction and courage. She came from the Kerpel family, and was the daughter of first cousins Leopold Kerpel and Johanna Reichfeld. Along with

Mutti, Leopold and Johanna had another two daughters, Erzi and Aranka, and a son called Max. Mutti grew up with her family in the small village of Mattersburg. I remember Papa used to call it *Matterstraf*, meaning 'Matters-punishment', because Grandmother Kerpel ruled the town with an iron fist.

Grandmother Kerpel was the driving force behind her family's wheat and flour business. She wasn't very tall, but she was remarkably lively and so commanded respect at the flourmill. Apparently, she had inherited her forthright qualities from her mother; I never met her but relatives told me stories. When first told of the invention of the telephone, she said indignantly: 'Old I am, but not so stupid to believe this nonsense!' She would sit by the window of her apartment, which was opposite the Kerpel business, and check when employees arrived and left, keeping note of who was on time. She kept a detailed mental taxonomy of who worked hard and who did not. She was the self-appointed supervisor of all matters of employment.

We spent many school holidays and sometimes Rosh Hashanah at the Kerpels'. Their house was simple but well kept. As you walked in from the street, there was a lounge, dining room and kitchen all in one large area. The bedrooms were off the kitchen, and out the back were some horses, goats and chickens. It was always spotless. Grandmother Kerpel ceaselessly had workers performing some type of repair. I felt right at home there. We could run around the street, gallivant, and enjoy the security of a smaller town.

I was also impressed that the Kerpel family was among the first in Mattersburg to have electricity. Grandmother Kerpel used to sit on an elevated stool in the middle of the family room under the sole electric bulb, which hung low from the ceiling. Illuminated and penetrating, she would recite German poetry by Schiller and Goethe. On *shabbat* she read the '*Tseno Ureno*', a liturgical poem composed at the end of the sixteenth century by Jacob Isaac Ashkenazi, and she gave the most energetic recitations of stories from the Torah. As a young girl, I loved watching her read. Her eyes focused on every line with a unique intensity.

Her husband, Grandfather Kerpel, was *rosh kehilah* for many years. All the community's problems came to him. I didn't see him much. He wasn't the sort of grandfather who would sit down and talk to you, but he did sing a lot, and I would sit and listen to him. I remember the way he sang '*Oyfn Pripetshik*' in a sweet but mournful tone.

Grandfather Kerpel had a brother called Shaya Baci. One Rosh Hashanah eve, when we were visiting Mattersburg, a false rumour went around the village that Shaya Baci had tragically died. Steadily, members of the community showed up at the Kerpels' house, offering condolences and asking my grandfather when the funeral would be. Fed up, he told them to come in – it was to be held then and there.

Shaya had dressed himself in a white sheet and was lying on the floor. Once everyone was assembled in the room, he launched his arms straight in the air and started to rise, as if coming back from the dead. Everyone was shouting, '*Gilgul! Gilgul!*'

Mattersburg was only a small town and did not have a school for higher education, so Mutti was sent to Hungary for her schooling. She stayed with her aunt, uncle and cousins, the Lowinger family. They were well known for their wit, intelligence and culture.

It was there that Mutti cultivated her taste for the piano, and she soon acquired a liking for and interest in the culture of classical music. During school holidays, on her way home from Hungary, she would stop off in Vienna to go shopping. She loved shopping. When she married my father, the village girl from Mattersburg effortlessly became one of Bratislava's most elegantly dressed women.

Mutti had excellent taste. She simply had that sense – to look at something and know immediately if it was quality. She had an instinct for fashion. She wore uneven hems and high heels, as well as a beautiful *sheitl*, and in winter there was usually a fox over her shoulder.

Her sense of taste was a point of great pride for Papa. He would encourage her to go and buy things for herself. She was more subservient than her mother, the tenacious Grandmother Kerpel. Papa was the boss. But Mutti's intelligence meant that she commanded respect. She was an avid reader, she wrote well-crafted stories and she maintained the household.

Every afternoon at Palisády 60, Papa and Mutti would play chess in the salon. In the left corner stood a huge oven heater that was covered with hand-painted ceramic tiles, its flue reaching all the way to the ceiling. Opposite the oven was a very wide red velvet lounge chair that converted into the bed where Kurti slept. The floor was polished wood, covered with an ornate Persian rug that somehow survived the devastation that was to come; it still lies on the floor in my house.

Every time I see that rug I'm reminded of Mutti and Papa and their lives at Palisády 60 – how Papa was always cleanly shaven, dressed like a modern man, and how Mutti would be draped in furs as they left to go to the theatre. How Papa would arrive home from business in another country laden with cantaloupes, bananas, dates, figs and other exotic fruits. I remember Mutti's hand-woven linen draping and the deep mahogany table in the dining room, the walls colourful with embroideries of flowers and landscapes, the crystal chandeliers hanging over my head at the table and the dark beige silk curtains, tied back formally with ribbon. I remember a vitrine filled with miniature filigree, silver dining tables and chairs, cups and saucers, all tiny and beautifully made. Sometimes I was allowed to play with these miniature items as a special treat.

*

This was the time of our lives that was, in its very essence, cosmopolitan. As a little girl, I would look out from the balcony of Palisády 60 into the presidential gardens that lay across the road. Directly opposite us was Café Stefanie, a popular meeting place for swish young Bratislavans. The sounds of their conversation and the smell of the cakes and coffee would sail over the street and fill me up. These images and scents were a part of my life – in a very real way, they were part of how I envisioned my future. But I was never allowed to eat the cakes from Café Stefanie as they were not kosher.

The grand bathtub at Palisády 60 had golden claw feet. There were live carp in it all week, which would be removed on the Thursday night. The next day we'd wash the tub, heat up some water, bathe and wash our hair, while the carp would be prepared for our *shabbat* meal. Before Papa would go to *shul* he would hide away all of his *muktzeh* items – his wallet, pens and business documents – by placing them in a white serviette, which was tied in a knot. Then, when he came home, he would bless us all by placing a serviette on our heads and saying a special prayer. It is clear to me now, as it was clear to me then: the real substance of our family life lay deep within our Jewishness.

Our kitchen was strictly kosher. Every night of the week a boy studying at the yeshivah would be fed dinner in our kitchen before Papa arrived home. Mutti was head of the kitchen. She koshered all the meat we ate herself, using a special tilted chopping board to drain the animal completely of its blood after the slaughter. After this, the meat had to soak for half an hour, then it was salted with coarse salt on all sides and left for one hour. After this process the meat was washed three times very thoroughly.

Mutti also did all of the cooking. Her food was excellent. I loved her goulash and potato gnocchi, which we called *schishkelach*. We also ate *nokkerln*, a gnocchi made from a base of flour and water and served with paprika chicken breast.

The most memorable meals, of course, were during *shabbat*. I would carry a big pot of *cholent* to the baker's oven on Friday afternoon, then I would pick it up with a maid on Saturday. The beans and smoked meat in the stew smelt almost sweet, and our dish would be wrapped in brown paper with 'Weiss' written on it. We would eat it with *challah* that Mutti baked specially.

The most delicious treats were Mutti's yeast cakes and strudel. There was the Viennese strudel that she stretched in her hands, held aloft, until it was thin enough to reach the length of the kitchen table. I remember the taste of the raw chestnuts Mutti pounded into a paste for her cakes. She sometimes served the raw paste sweetened with chocolate cream as a treat for the family.

There was a huge pantry at the far end of the kitchen. In winter, it would get so cold that Mutti would freeze raw goose fat there overnight. I would sprinkle the frozen lard with paprika and spread it on dark bread. It had a flavour I've not since tasted, but have often craved. When I was pregnant with my first child, I had a great desire for this frozen fat. I was in Australia by then, and the only lard available was from chicken fat. I put it in the freezer, sprinkled it with paprika and ate it on bread. I was sick for two straight days afterwards.

A Premonition

Palisády Ulica, Bratislava, 1938

Palisády 60 was my playground. There was a small courtyard garden that was surrounded by trellises, which in summer would become heavy with ripe grapes. And there was also an attic, where my cousins and I played soldiers, dress-ups and board games among the drying clothes. One afternoon my cousins and I took the older women's sanitary pads, which were made from cloth, from the washing lines. We placed them on our heads and marched around the building like we were an army wearing special caps.

We also played in the *Kinderzimmer*, or nursery, which was adjacent to our parents' bedroom. Its window looked out over our garden. Below the windowsill was a coal-burning stove with a flat surface, on which our nanny, Maria Wohlschlager, heated soup for us on cold winter days when we came home from school.

Maria was from Germany so we'd speak German with her and each other. At school we studied and spoke in Slovakian, as it was the official language. We spoke German with Papa and Mutti, but they spoke Hungarian with each other whenever they didn't want us to understand them.

The Jewish community in Bratislava had two day schools. One was Orthodox, and so very traditional, and the other was Neologue, or progressive. We attended the Orthodox school, which was a fifteen-minute walk from our home. Our uniform was a white shirt, a navy-blue skirt, and woollen stockings and galoshes in winter.

In summer the walk to school was pleasant enough, but in winter the snow was fierce. Even with our galoshes, woollen stockings and fur muffs and hats it was bone-achingly cold. We came home crying every day, wet to our knees from the snow. We would hurriedly rip off our wet outer clothes and leave them at the front door, then run to the warm stove in the *Kinderzimmer*, where we'd warm our hands and bellies with a bowl of hot soup.

*

Rabbi Schreiber was the chief rabbi of Bratislava; his daughter, Thea, went to school with us. They lived in one of the most elegant apartments in Bratislava. Sometimes we'd be invited for a hot chocolate in the afternoon.

A Premonition

I remember my father asking Rabbi Schreiber, when the trouble started, whether we should go to Palestine.

'No,' he said, 'the Mashiach will come to Bratislava.'

Later on, he himself managed to escape with his family to Palestine.

Although we went to the Orthodox school, the Jewish community we were part of was modern, not Hasidic, and we lived a very good life. We were sophisticated. On Sunday afternoons couples would *schpazier* on the Korzo, the main walkway by the Danube. The women would wear full fur or foxes draped over their shoulders, and hats and gloves. Their husbands would wear fashionable coats and hats. They walked side by side, nodding politely to other couples that walked past.

Our *shul* was ornately decorated with specially carved wood. The women sat upstairs behind a curtain, and would dress in their best clothes. There was, of course, an element of pride and competitiveness.

Because Kurti was our family's only son, he had private lessons in Hebrew and Torah everyday with Rabbi Einhorn. Einhorn had the thickest fingers I had ever seen, and he didn't hesitate to give Kurti a clip behind the ears if his attention strayed for even a moment. We girls were not allowed into the room but stood with our ears glued to the door in the hope of learning something.

Kurti was a bookworm. Papa was priming him to take over the family business, but Kurti would hide under a table or behind a couch and just read all day. His great passion was reading and writing Hebrew poetry. This literary love was fuelled by his most ardent desire: to make *aliyah*, to live in Palestine as soon as possible.

His Zionism developed from going to the youth movement Bnei Akiva, of which I was also a member. What I learned was how to hope for a brighter future for the Jewish people. To this day, I believe that it was my ability to hope for a better life in Palestine that sustained me during my darkest times at Auschwitz.

So strong was my belief that, when I was eight years of age, I went to the Bnei Akiva immigration department, alone, and registered to move to Palestine. My parents, understandably, would not allow it. Later on, they bitterly regretted their decision.

But how were they to know? How was anyone to know? Our lives at Palisády 60 were happy and fulfilling. We lived with one foot in the Jewish practices of our ancestors and another foot in the modern, secular world. Maria would take us to the park every afternoon, and we would play with our non-Jewish friends and neighbours. We would play as regular children everywhere play. I felt like I belonged.

My life was filled with family, Jewishness, happiness, abundance. I sometimes wonder why, as an eight-year-old, I had a desire to be elsewhere, to be in Palestine. Perhaps I had felt some faint premonitory darkness of the long nightmare that was awaiting us.

Invasion

Palisády Ulica, Bratislava, 1939

It was just before *Pesach*, March 1939. The weather was beautiful. My parents were playing chess and I was in the dining room, playing with my silver figurines. Suddenly, we were interrupted by an unfamiliar sound.

Threatening noises came through the window. Drums beating, boots pounding in regular rhythm. There was chanting in the distance. I rushed to the window and saw the German army, rigid with rifles, marching into Bratislava. They were singing: *'Denn heute gehört uns Deutschland und Morgen die ganze Welt'* – Today Germany is ours, and tomorrow the whole world.

Our nanny, Maria, ran into the dining room. When she saw the Germans she danced with joy. Her slightly cross-eyed stare was wet with emotion. 'I have lived to see this great day,' she screamed, elated. Her fist was raised in some sort of victory salute.

I was confused. My nanny, the woman with whom I shared a room, was ecstatic, while my parents, who had hired her, were mortified. I didn't know what to think.

*

There had been warning signs. In 1938 Mutti's parents, Johanna and Leopold, together with their other daughters, Erzi and Aranka, arrived on our doorstep. They had no luggage and no money. They had been evicted from their house in Mattersburg and made the journey to Bratislava.

A few days later Mutti's older brother, Max, arrived with his wife, Roszi. He was angry. He hated Bratislava. He kept saying to Papa, 'Jeno, they hate us here like they hated us in Austria. We must move to Palestine before it is too late.'

Papa nodded and gave Max and Roszi the money they needed for a boat to Haifa, as they were penniless.

I was mystified. Why were they going and we staying? If it was too dangerous for Max and Roszi, surely it was too dangerous for us?

I began hearing stories of Jews being beaten on the streets. Our neighbours and even our friends not only turned their backs to us, they actually expressed a deep hatred for us, as if we were not human. When I greeted my friends – with whom

I had played in the park just a month or so before – they turned their heads away as if they didn't know me. I felt like shouting, 'I'm one of you! My parents, my grandparents were born here!' But they had suddenly learnt how to hate us.

It took a few weeks for Max and Roszi to start their new life in Tel Aviv. Papa wrote to Max, asking if he would sponsor Mutti's parents on a journey to Palestine. Roszi flatly refused the responsibility, so we were left to look after Papa's parents and Mutti's parents. Being the oldest daughter, I spent a great deal of time caring for them. I cleaned for them, maintained their health, took them food.

At night I would lie in bed and imagine Uncle Max and Roszi in Tel Aviv. I felt resentment towards them, towards everyone. I often wondered to myself what Uncle Max had meant when he said 'before it's too late'. How much worse could it get?

*

Three days after Bratislava was invaded, the Hlinka Guard, the Slovak counterparts of the SS, began marching through the streets, arresting and harassing Jews.

It was a sunny spring day but I was in bed, sick with diphtheria. I heard banging and shouting coming from downstairs in my grandparents' apartment. I got out of bed to find Mutti and ask her what was happening. She was standing in the entrance hall of our apartment and looked frightened.

Suddenly, the front door of our apartment was thrown open and a gang of young men from the Hlinka Guard barged in, holding Pres Opapa under the shoulders. They threw him on the floor. His face was covered in blood. 'This is what will happen to you if you don't toe the line!' they shouted, then they left.

We helped Pres Opapa to his feet and took him to the bathroom to clean him. He told us that the Hlinka Guard had broken in to his apartment and beaten him in front of Pres Omama. They had broken his front teeth and tied his gold pocket watch around his neck, before dragging him upstairs to our apartment.

A few days later, when I was still in bed sick, the Hlinka Guard broke into our apartment again, and this time they arrested Papa. They were rounding up many of the prominent and wealthy members of the Jewish community, holding them for ransom at an inner-city prison.

Suddenly, Mutti was alone. She had to look after a house full of loved ones and cope with the terror of her husband's arrest. She was accustomed to Papa looking after everything, but now his life was her responsibility.

The very next day Mutti woke early, fed us breakfast and got dressed in her best clothes. As she was walking out of the front door I noticed she wasn't wearing a *sheitl*. I wanted to ask her why, but something made me hold my tongue. I was perplexed. She was moving with a fearful intensity.

Mutti was searching for a buyer for the building we owned in the middle of the city, Papa's shop. She didn't wear her *sheitl* because it made her appear too Jewish. She had little commercial knowledge and no clue as to how much the shop was worth. But through her natural intelligence and will – and through necessity – she managed to sell the building for a decent price.

Mutti used the money from the sale to bribe the SS for Papa's release. We were among the lucky ones. Many of those arrested in those early days were sent to Dachau, and their ashes later returned to their families.

*

That first week after the invasion was the worst of my life. It was as if I had gone to sleep one night, happy and secure at Palisády 60, and then in the morning I had awoken to a nightmare.

During that first week, I saw Pres Opapa beaten, Papa arrested and Mutti a changed woman. It was during this week that I ceased to be a child; I lost my innocence forever.

I don't remember crying to anyone, but my internal world was filled with a constant and bewildered weeping. Nothing would be simple or calm or easy ever again.

Why Didn't We Leave?

PALISÁDY ULICA, BRATISLAVA, 1941

My sister Renata was born in March 1941. She was a very sweet baby and she brought our family a lot of joy. There was little joy, however, for the wider community of Jews in Bratislava.

Edict after edict stripped us of our most basic rights. Our bank accounts were frozen, and our jewellery, paintings and silver – including our treasured candlesticks – were confiscated. We were forced to wear the humiliating yellow star, and all debts owing to us were annulled.

These events, the persecution of my people, have become part of the collection of facts that people now call 'history'. I lived these facts every day. They are part of my memory.

'History' tells us that the Jews of Bratislava were persecuted by the invading Nazis. What it doesn't tell us is how it feels, as a nine-year-old girl, to have your bicycle forced from your hands,

Why Didn't We Leave?

confiscated by a soldier while your father watches, powerless. And all for a reason so hateful – so base, so inhumane – that he cannot possibly explain it to you, let alone to himself.

*

Why didn't we leave? The question hangs over this period of my life like a dark cloud. Was Papa blind to what was going on around him? There were times when I thought this might be the case.

One day Kurti came home from school with bruises around his eyes and a cut mouth. When Papa arrived home Kurti ran up to him and said, 'Papa, I was beaten up on my way to school.'

Papa looked upset but replied, 'Kurti, this was an isolated incident. You will walk to school again tomorrow and everything will be fine.'

The next day, I quietly followed Kurti when he left for school. I stayed around a hundred yards behind him so he wouldn't see me. As he turned down a small alley, I saw a group of Hitler Youth waiting for him. He turned around and tried to run away.

The boys caught up to him. They circled him, threw him to the floor, kicked him in the ribs and face. Then they took his bag and strewed its contents all over the street.

When at last they left him alone, Kurti quietly got back to his feet, repacked his bag, put on his hat and continued to school, just as Papa had asked of him.

I ran home and told my parents what I had seen.

'This is just a bad period of time for us,' Papa said. 'Things will get better.'

*

The prime minister of Slovakia, Vojtech Tuka, used to go for long walks down Štefánikova Ulica, which ran perpendicular to Palisády Ulica. He was a Catholic and a great admirer of Hitler.

One day I was walking down Štefánikova Ulica, heading for home. I was trying to hide my humiliating yellow star by walking with my hand over my chest.

I saw Tuka walking towards me. I recognised his face, as I had seen him walk in the Presidential Park opposite our home on many occasions. He looked menacing with his shiny black boots and grey ponytail. *Why is Tuka staring at me?* I wondered. *Maybe I'm just imagining it?* But no, he had noticed that I was trying to hide the yellow star.

When Tuka had come within three steps of me we both stopped. We looked at each other for a moment. I was transfixed by something hateful in his eyes.

Suddenly, he grabbed me by the arm, revealing my yellow star. I trembled under his grasp. He wrenched me towards him and kicked me in the stomach with his boot. I was winded and fell to the ground. He stood over me and shouted, 'There, little

Jewish girl, you can get up now. Let everyone see your star.'

Passers-by smiled and nodded their approval.

I jumped on a passing tram and sat down, forgetting that Jews were no longer permitted to sit on public transport. Immediately, an elderly woman opposite me yelled out, 'Look at that Jewish girl sitting down – what nerve! Get out!' I stood up quickly, but all the other passengers joined her in chasing me off the tram.

Is this story hard to believe? It seems, in a way, beyond belief. But why should it be believable? This was a time when the unthinkable, the unbelievable, became my reality. Is it believable that, at the same time, Jews were being sent in packed trains for extermination?

*

Was Papa blind to our persecution? No. No one could have been blind to the suffering we endured. Papa was a man of principle and, as always, he was trying to find a solution.

Papa was too astute, too intelligent, to be accused of short-sightedness when it came to the Nazis' intentions. If he had been blind, he wouldn't have immediately arranged a boat to take Mutti's sisters and his employees to Palestine. Nor would he have started working behind the counter in the shop, so he could meet customers who might become contacts that could help him hide his family.

After Mutti's sisters made their trip to Palestine, we received a letter from them, describing how treacherous their journey had been. The ship was overcrowded, people weren't fed properly, the sick became sicker and the boat almost sank. At that moment, Papa realised that his elderly parents could never make the journey to Palestine.

There are certain principles that, if broken, make life no longer worth living. We stayed in Bratislava because of my father's devotion to his mother and father. If we had left, he would have been overwhelmed by guilt.

So that's the answer. We stayed and things became worse.

Loss

Judengasse, Bratislava, Winter 1941

As the snow started to fall in 1941, Mutti's father was diagnosed with lung cancer. He was sent to the Jewish hospital across town. Mutti and I would catch the tram to visit him there.

One afternoon, Mutti went alone to see her father. He knew he was approaching death, and he had one final request. 'I crave the taste of a red apple,' he told her.

A few days later, Mutti and I were walking in the city. Suddenly, she stopped at a stall that displayed piles of beautiful apples. She stared longingly at the fruit.

'What's the matter?' I asked.

'Papa wants an apple, but we don't have enough money on us to buy it and take the tram to the hospital. If we are to give it to him, we will have to walk.'

By this time it was dangerous for Jews to walk the streets, but nevertheless we chose the apple and the long walk. Grandfather Kerpel's dying wish, such a modest final request, was fulfilled, and he passed away shortly after.

*

After Mutti's father's death, we all slumped into a deep mourning, but particularly his widow, Johanna. She told my parents that she wanted some space in which to grieve her loss. My parents arranged for her to live in a one-bedroom flat with a kitchenette and an outside toilet. It was in the Jewish Ghetto, known as the Judengasse.

Mutti did not want her mother to live alone, so I was told I was to leave Palisády 60 and keep Grandmother Kerpel company. I was to help with whatever she needed to be done. Although the apartment was tiny compared to Palisády 60, I loved it.

My grandmother and I were very different, but we respected each other. She allowed me to roam the streets as I pleased. It was the first time in my life that I had experienced such independence, and I enjoyed it.

Together we started a small business. In our tiny kitchenette, we would bake biscuits made of nuts and topped with meringue – they were called *Nuschtangel*. I mixed the icing sugar with a fork for what seemed like hours to make it smooth and spreadable. Placing the delicate meringues on the nut base was precarious; sometimes they would break. Grandmother would shout, 'Look what we've done!' and then weep. I was secretly quite happy, though, because I could then eat the broken *Nuschtangel*.

When they were ready, Grandmother would tie the biscuits up in small parcels and I would deliver them by foot to delicatessens and cafés throughout the city. As I weaved my way through Bratislava's streets, I would hold the parcels as if they were crown jewels. With the money we earned, we could afford some delicacies: butter, bread and even pickled cucumbers.

I used to visit my family in Palisády Ulica quite often. I missed my siblings terribly. One afternoon I went to visit them and, as I opened the door to our apartment, I saw Papa talking to a man I had never met before. Papa saw me and said, 'This is Mr Krampl. He is the new owner of the business.'

Mr Krampl was an illiterate peasant with no connection to our family. He was an *arizátor*, someone who had been granted ownership of a Jewish business by the Nazis.

As the *arizátor* of the business, Mr Krampl could request the exemption from deportation of a Jew and his immediate family if the Jew was required to run the business. These 'protected Jews' were issued with special exemption certificates that were valid until such time that he or she was no longer needed.

Mr Krampl used Papa and Uncle David to run the business in return for their lives. He paid them meagre wages, which then had to be paid in taxes and penalties to the Nazis.

Papa, a man with such a keen business mind, was no longer working for money or to develop his business, but simply to keep his young family from deportation. It was an impossible situation.

*

Things soon became worse: Uncle David received orders from the Nazi authorities that he and his family had to leave Palisády 60 and move to a Jewish transit house on Budkova Ulica.

When Papa heard the news he ran upstairs to David and Frida. 'You have to go into hiding immediately,' he told them. 'I have arranged spots throughout Hungary and Slovakia for you and the children.'

Auntie Frida would not hear of it. 'Jeno, I'm not going to live somewhere that doesn't have a maid,' she said.

Uncle David assured Papa they would be okay at Budkova Ulica. 'Anyway,' he added, 'we have our exemption certificates from Mr Krampl.'

In early 1942, the SS broke into Uncle David's house at Budkova in the middle of the night and arrested his family. David showed them his exemption certificate, his last hope of salvation, but it was ripped up before his eyes. Mr Krampl had secretly denounced David, who was no longer deemed necessary in the functioning of the business. His family had been made redundant.

My father heard news of David's arrest and was stricken by panic. He was willing to bribe anyone, to do anything for their release, but no one would touch his money.

Mr Krampl saw my father's desperation, his pain, his hopelessness, his grief. 'I don't understand you Jews,' he said. 'You are such cowards. I was at the dentist this morning, had two fillings and endured the pain like a soldier.'

We received one more letter from Auntie Frida: 'Look after yourselves,' she wrote. 'Wish we would have followed your advice. Ruti has high temperature. Worried about her well-being. Love, Frida.' It was sent from Žilina, where there was a labour camp.

From Žilina they were deported to Sereď, from Sereď they were sent to Lublin, and from Lublin they were sent to Auschwitz. We never heard from them again.

Duty

From the Judengasse back to Palisády 60, Summer 1942

After he denounced Uncle David, Mr Krampl immediately moved his family into Palisády 60. I was still living with Grandmother Kerpel in the Judengasse. I did not see much of my parents at this time, but my sisters told me that Papa spent a lot of his time weeping.

One afternoon I went to visit my parents at Palisády 60. There were bags everywhere. 'What's happening?' I asked Papa.

'We're being moved to Budkova,' he said.

'Like Uncle David?' I asked, panicking.

Papa shook his head and led me down to the cellar. He pointed to the ground, made of solid concrete. 'Under this concrete I have buried certificates that prove that we once owned all the things that the Germans have taken away from us. One day, when this ends, we will be able to have them back.

'More importantly, I have buried the things that draw closest to the soul of our family. There are birth certificates, photographs of your grandparents, documents of all kinds. I've also buried a *sefer Torah*. When this ends, we will come back and dig these things up. Our family and our traditions will be preserved.'

After my family was evicted from Palisády 60 and moved to Budkova Ulica, Papa was enlisted into forced labour. He spent his days building trenches and his nights working for Mr Krampl.

Illegal arrests and deportations were regular. Entire families were taken in the middle of the night, never to be heard from again. Papa was suspicious of Mr Krampl and did not want to rely on his exemption certificate for our protection. Uncle David's loss was with him always.

He arranged hiding places for all of us children. At Budkova it often happened that my siblings were woken up by Mutti and Papa and told to run to hiding spots when they thought they were going to be arrested.

I did not have to hide because I was living with Grandmother Kerpel, and our address wasn't registered. Despite this, Papa worried that something bad would happen to us living alone in the Judengasse. So we were separated: he arranged for Grandmother Kerpel to be smuggled to Budapest and put into hiding. With a heavy heart I said goodbye to my beloved grandmother, Johanna. I didn't know it then, but I would never see her again.

*

Shortly after my family was moved to Budkova Ulica, I was sent back to Palisády 60 by Papa to look after his elderly parents. Jews were forbidden to employ non-Jewish help. I was put in charge of every aspect of my grandparents' care. I was ten years of age.

I was woken nightly by their cries and lamentations. Pres Omama would complain, '*Die linke Niere tut mir weh*' – My left kidney is hurting me. Then Pres Opapa would moan, '*Mein rechter Bauch tut mir weh*' – The right side of my stomach is hurting me. I would jump up and give them both various pills. My feet would be numb with cold by the time I got back into bed. Falling asleep again was impossible.

Pres Opapa got up early, around five in the morning, and lit the stove before Pres Omama and I got out of bed. He was very caring, despite being overcome by illness and anxiety. He tried to hide this from me. He bought us fresh rolls for breakfast, and sometimes milk when it was available. When I accompanied Pres Omama to the local market I had to carry her large wicker basket, as our maid had once done.

I spent all my time with my elderly grandparents, and I missed my siblings terribly. I did not feel appreciated.

Duty

*

Jewish ritual slaughter was banned in Bratislava, and my parents refused to eat non-kosher meat. One day Mutti took me by the hand and said, 'Darling, you do not look Jewish. It is now your job to take chickens to the *shochet*. I'm sorry that we have to put you through this.'

When I brought the slaughtered chickens home to my grandparents, I had to clean them, feathers and all, and then *kasher* them. Was I a maid or their granddaughter? I sometimes wondered.

Just before Rosh Hashanah in 1942, I was given a large goose to take to slaughter. The goose was placed in a large bag with a zip on top, which was left slightly ajar for air. I think that goose was heavier than me. I began dragging it through the streets of Bratislava to its death.

Suddenly, when I was in the Kapucínska Gasse, the bag started trembling. I wondered if the goose was struggling for air. I put the bag down and opened the zip a little more.

The goose poked its long neck through the zip and looked at me. I was startled and took a step back, then watched helplessly as the huge bird stepped out of the bag and waddled away, between the legs of passers-by. I was too scared to try to catch it.

I came home empty-handed, leaving four families without meat for Rosh Hashanah.

*

It is a lonely thing to feel unappreciated. I was so occupied with Papa's parents that I hardly had time to wash. They tried to look after me, in their own way. But they were old and sick.

I felt rewarded, though, when Pres Omama gave me a gold ring bearing my initials, 'EW'. She'd had it specially made for my eleventh birthday.

Can You Hear Us?

Dobrovičova, Bratislava, Yom Kippur 1942

I was reunited with my parents and siblings a few days before Yom Kippur in 1942. We were relocated to Dobrovičova Ulica, along with some other Jews. Eighteen adults and children shared one small flat. It was guarded by a *Hausmeister*, who would stand outside our door to prevent us from escaping.

He was evil; I was told stories about him. If his wife gave birth to a daughter, he would kill her and hide her body in the attic.

Mutti managed to find one chicken before the Yom Kippur fast that year. I watched how she divided the meat to make it last.

She boiled the chicken into a soup and filled Papa's parents' bowls with the thick, rich broth. Then she filled the pot with water and served the youngest children, filled the pot again and fed the visitors, diluted it still more and fed us older children, and then finally she served herself and Papa.

What they were drinking was no more than hot water.

*

Pres Opapa and Pres Omama became weaker and weaker. Papa knew that they would not have the strength to make it into hiding if the Hlinka Guard came to arrest us. Their presence was endangering our whole family. With a heavy heart, Papa placed his parents in two different hospitals, in order to protect them from deportation.

It was still my duty to care for them. Every morning I would walk to Pres Opapa's hospital. I would help him walk around the room. Then I'd stare out the window and into the courtyard below.

That part of the hospital was a mental institution. The patients would spend their days walking in circles in the yard. Among them I recognised the faces of Jews, people who were not mentally ill. They were hiding in the hospital, feigning madness.

At one pm I would leave Pres Opapa and walk to Pres Omama's hospital. She was in a ward with eight beds.

One afternoon, Pres Omama was crying when I arrived. 'What's wrong, Omama?' I asked.

'They gave me an injection,' she replied. 'I can no longer walk.'

Can You Hear Us?

Every day I nursed her and emptied her bedpan. I also looked after the other patients in the ward, as this was the condition under which Pres Omama had been allowed to stay at that hospital.

Pres Omama received a fresh roll at dinnertime and always hid it under her blanket. She would give it to me when I came to visit her the next day. I gladly accepted it – I was always so hungry. There was hardly any food at Dobrovičova.

*

One night, a truck pulled up in front of our crowded flat. Mutti, who at this time was heavily pregnant with my sister Ruth, looked out of the window. She turned to us, ashen-faced. 'The Hlinka Guard have come to arrest us!' she said. She looked at us a moment longer, then lay down on the bed.

'What are you doing, Mutti?' we cried. 'Get up! We must hide!'

The Hlinka Guard beat down our door. Everyone froze. Suddenly, Mutti went into spasms, choking fits, breathlessness and hysteria, throwing herself onto the floor and wailing.

We said, 'Mutti, *emet, emet?*' which in Hebrew means, 'Is this real?' Mutti did not respond but continued her convulsions, now making horrendous choking sounds.

We did not know what to do. Neither did the thugs from the Hlinka Guard. We all stood staring at Mutti for a few moments.

In the confusion, the soldiers went to find help. Mutti immediately regained her normal state. 'Quick,' she said, 'let's run and hide.'

On another occasion it was my father who saw the terrifying truck pull up outside our house. 'They're here!' he shouted. 'Quick, jump out the window and run to Maria Wohlschlager's!'

Without hesitating, Noemi and I jumped out of the window. It felt like a considerable height and I was dazed when I hit the ground.

When I regained my composure I felt someone holding my arm. It was Noemi. She tugged it. 'Look, Eva!' We were surrounded by the Hlinka Guard. There were at least five of them, their guns pointing at us.

They dragged us out to the front of our flat. Our whole family was lined up, waiting to be loaded onto the truck.

Out of the darkness a German voice shouted, 'Attention, come here!' All the soldiers followed the voice into the darkness. In that moment Papa yelled, 'Run!' and we all managed to scatter and flee to our hiding places.

These were the ways – a seizure, a voice in the night – in which we were saved from deportation.

Not all families were as lucky as we were. Months earlier, on the night of *Pesach*, Uncle Shamu, Aunt Dina and their children were arrested in Dunajská Streda. They were dragged away from the *seder* table, still clutching the second cup of wine.

They were deported to a concentration camp in Poland. After a little while we received a card from Dina: 'Shamu has been sent to the *shochet*. The rest of us will be there shortly.'

We never heard from them again.

*

Jewish holidays were favourite times for deportation, gassing and torture. Were they mocking our faith? Did that, too, have to be attacked?

The rabbis of Bratislava issued an edict that we include in our daily prayers the *Avinu Malkeinu*. We recited it every morning: *Our Father, our King. Hear our voice!*

Did You hear me those mornings? *Our Father, our King. Have compassion upon us, upon our children!*

Bombs fell on Bratislava. We would hear the sirens and run for shelter. *Our Father, our King. Bring an end to pestilence, war and famine.*

During one raid, I sat with my family in a shelter. We were safe from the bombs, but not from being denounced. A young boy, no older than six, sat by himself in the corner, shaking. He had no family. He looked Jewish. Everyone in the shelter stared at him.

The bombs fell around us. *Our Father, our King. Bring an end to the trouble and oppression around us.* And then the bombs stopped.

The Jewish boy stood up quickly. One of the Slovaks had been eyeing him, and stood up too. The little boy started to run towards the exit. The man caught him by the arm. 'Jew!' he shouted as he dragged him away.

Our Father, our King. Can you hear us?

Our Father, our King. Can you hear the boy's screams? I can.

The Ghetto

Klariská Ulica, Bratislava, Spring 1943

In April 1943 we were sent from Dobrovičova to Klariská Ulica, a type of Jewish ghetto. We received a letter saying: 'Your request to move to Klariská has been approved.' We had made no such request.

Pres Opapa and Pres Omama were still in the public hospitals. One day I went to visit them and noticed that all the Jewish people hiding among the mentally insane had disappeared. I told Papa, and straightaway he moved my grandparents in with us at Klariská. They slept in the beds and the rest of us slept on the floor.

In Klariská our flat was tiny. There was one cold-water tap for cooking and washing, and one external toilet for almost eighty people.

Shortly after we moved there, Pres Omama became very ill. She was suffering from large kidney stones. The doctors told us there was no hope, and Omama knew she was at the end. She told me about her fear of dying. 'I'm terrified of worms nibbling at me,' she said, 'of being in the ground summer and winter, devoured by worms.'

One afternoon a group of men from the *chevrah kadishah* arrived to say *vidui*, asking forgiveness on her behalf. She was close to death but still semi-conscious. Her eyes were stark and fearful. It seemed to me that treating someone as passed who has not yet passed was an act of profound cruelty.

Pres Omama died shortly after. She was buried in the Jewish cemetery.

*

Mutti gave birth to my sister Ruth during the time we were staying in Klariská Ulica. The doctors and nurses at the Charitas Hospital would only assist Mutti with the delivery on the condition that she agreed to leave the hospital straight after the birth. What choice did she have?

With Renata in the pram, I went to pick up Mutti. I waited outside the hospital. Mutti walked out holding my new baby sister. She leaned heavily on the pram during the walk home.

Not long afterwards, I became sick. I constantly felt weak and fatigued. One day Mutti took my hand. She winced when she saw how my wrists had become swollen and discoloured.

'Eva' she said quietly, 'we must take you to a doctor.' I was

The Ghetto

diagnosed with rheumatic fever, and I had to have my tonsils removed.

It was against the law for Jews to have procedures performed in hospitals. But there was a Jewish ear, nose and throat professor whom the Germans had spared because of his brilliance. He agreed to operate on me.

'I will perform this operation if, and only if, Eva follows my instructions,' he said. 'She must walk straight into the operating theatre, not through the hospital admittance desk. I will perform the operation and then she must leave immediately. There will be no time for recovery and absolutely no visits.'

The next day my parents walked me to the hospital. A few metres before the entrance I felt Mutti's hand slip from mine. I was on my own. I kept walking.

The Jewish surgeon told me that my tonsils and adenoids were to be removed under local anaesthetic. I was seated upright in a dentist's chair. There were two Catholic nuns in the room with us. I was shaking with fear.

The surgeon was stern. He asked one of the nuns to pass him a needle with the anaesthetic. 'Open wide,' he said, and I obeyed. I felt the needle press against my gums. He applied pressure but could not break the skin. He pushed harder still, then noticed the tears streaming from my eyes.

He withdrew the needle, inspected it and then turned to the nun. 'What were you thinking?' he shouted. 'This is a blunt needle!'

She looked at him blankly. 'So what? She is Jewish.'

The doctor had to make do. He handed me a kidney bowl and told me to hold it in front of my face, to catch the blood that would come from my mouth and nose. I was so scared that I tried to get up from the chair and run away. The professor boxed me with his elbow back into the seat. He was operating against the law. I was not supposed to be there. Both our lives were in danger.

I could see the whole procedure through the mirror on his head. I watched as he put a sharp instrument down my throat and scooped out my tonsils.

At some point towards the end of the procedure, a group of SS soldiers charged through the door. 'You!' they shouted.

I thought they had come for me, but they grabbed the professor by his collar and dragged him away.

The nuns behaved as if nothing had happened. They wrenched me over to the washbasin. 'Wash off that blood and get out!'

That was fine with me. I had wanted to leave even before I arrived.

I ran out of the back of the hospital and saw my parents sitting on the curb. I flew into their arms, sobbing, not only in pain but bearing the horrible weight of guilt: had I been instrumental in the professor's arrest?

I was so weak that I could hardly stand. Papa asked a passing nun if I could rest somewhere in the hospital for a little while.

'Absolutely not!' she said.

The Ghetto

We walked back to Klariská Ulica.

Mutti tried everything to relieve my pain. Miraculously, she found some ice cream. It was the best thing that had happened to me for a long time.

*

The *Hausmeister* at Klariská Ulica was strict. He lived with his wife and his son, Ivan. They made sure we obeyed the six pm curfew and that we wore our Jewish stars at all times.

I was in charge of collecting our food rations: sugar, flour and milk. I would put Ruth and Renata in a pram and take them with me to the shop. Dragging the pram up and down the stairs was difficult for a young, undernourished girl.

The only milk we could get was watered down and went sour after one day, but I loved the sour milk. At Klariská there were no typical meals. We ate what was available.

There was an old people's home for Jews next door to us in the ghetto. It was where we would pray on *shabbat* and on Jewish holidays. Every evening, Papa would take me to help him change the old people into their nightwear before sleep. I would also feed them their meagre dinner.

Papa took Mutti's beautiful nightdresses and gave them away so that the old people had nightgowns. He also made me give away half of our weekly milk rations. I was so hungry, and I resented his generosity.

'You must respect the elderly,' he would say to me. 'You children are more resilient than them. One day you will be old and frail.'

When I distributed the milk among the old people I would secretly take a few sips. It was sour and delicious. But still I was constantly hungry.

The bombing raids were now more frequent. One night, around dinnertime, the siren went off and we ran to the shelter. As always, I shook with fear. The airplanes flew very low and our building shook; windows shattered and smoke engulfed us. The petrol refinery was hit and was on fire.

Suddenly, Mutti yelled out, 'Our dinner!' and ran out of the bomb shelter. She had left it cooking on the stove. That food was all we had to eat. It was too valuable to let it go to waste.

My Jewish school was occasionally still open. We were not allowed a blackboard or dictionaries, so learning became all but impossible. Our headmaster, Dr König, taught us geography by pointing to different parts of his body as though he were a map, because those too were forbidden. He tried his best to act as if things were normal. Throughout our lessons he would always be looking at the door, as if the SS were about to come in and drag him away.

And one night they did: all our teachers and their families were arrested and deported. We woke up the next morning and the school was closed. That was the end of my education for a while.

The Ghetto

*

One afternoon, Mr Stern, who wore his hat slanted, knocked on our door at Klariská Ulica. 'Please, can you help me?' he asked. 'I need a family to look after my sister-in-law, Miriam. She has become impossible for me.'

Mr Stern was powerful and well connected, so my parents agreed. This was not an easy decision. They already had too many mouths to feed.

Miriam was a bit older than me, but a lot taller and more robust. She was quite wild. She told my sisters and me about sex, contraceptives and other things that I couldn't really understand. My parents were horrified.

One morning Mutti and Papa were panicking. 'The money has gone! Where is the money! Have you seen it?' We looked everywhere. This money was the last thousand American dollars they had put away for emergencies.

My parents had a feeling that Miriam was the thief. 'Miriam, did you take our money? Just tell us where it is and everything will be okay.'

Miriam looked at them. 'But I did not take it,' she said, 'so I can't tell you where it is.'

Papa offered her a reward if she could find the money. She sat in her chair and thought a while. After a few minutes she got up and walked to the rubbish tins at the entrance to the building. There, stashed under one of the tins, was all one thousand dollars. A day later the rubbish was collected. Those savings would have been lost forever.

Miriam wasn't the only person we hid with us at Klariská. Like at Dobrovičova Ulica, at one point there were eighteen of us sleeping under that one tiny roof.

Mutti and Papa slept on the floor in the kitchen. One night I overheard them talking about how hard it was to keep everyone in order, to look after everyone. 'We are doing the right thing,' Mutti said. 'But for the grace of God, it could've been us on the run.'

Among those hiding at our place was Romi Cohn, a young boy who had escaped the SS in Bratislava and joined the partisans. He was ten years old. He survived the war and later wrote a book called *The Youngest Partisan.*

There was also Mr and Mrs Radec. One time Mr Radec was running a very high fever and had bulging abscesses on his neck. Mutti bathed the abscesses with hot salty water and burst them with a sewing needle that she sterilised by lighting a match under it. They survived and later settled in Australia with their two daughters.

Pres Opapa's sister – Auntie Fanny – also hid under our roof. Her hiding place was an empty cupboard that was invisible to the naked eye. Every time there was a knock at the door she bolted for the cupboard.

One day when I was in bed, feverish with pleurisy, my friend Trude from across the street came to visit. I lay in bed while Trude poked around the apartment.

'What's in here?' she asked, as she opened a cupboard in the kitchen. It seemed as though she were looking for something.

Trude started to open all the cupboards in our tiny apartment. She stopped in front of Auntie Fanny's hiding place. Her eyes squinted and she found the latch that opened it.

Trude flung open the door. Auntie Fanny was standing there, her eyes wide, stiff as a board. She collapsed onto Trude and they both fell to the ground. Auntie Fanny's wig fell off and she lay on Trude, stiff and bareheaded. 'It's a ghost!' Trude shouted, picking herself up and running from the house. She never returned.

Trude was a Jewish collaborator, promised freedom by the Nazis if she denounced other Jews. But she met the same fate as the Jews she gave up when she was sent to Auschwitz. On arrival, she was taken off the train and murdered by the Jewish *kapos*.

Who Will Live and Who Will Die?

KLARISKÁ ULICA, BRATISLAVA, YOM KIPPUR 1943

On Yom Kippur the community was lamenting with fervour in the old people's home. The *Unnetaneh Tokef* sounded different this year. *Who will live and who die? Who by fire and who by sword?* The old men cried for atonement.

Through the cries came a knock at the door. It was the SS. At gunpoint they ordered the congregation into the yard.

In the yard there was a live pig that the SS had bought along. We were lined up in front of the pig. The *Hausmeister* of our apartment building in Klariská was standing there. One of the SS men handed him a knife. 'Slaughter it!' he ordered, and a slow shudder passed through the crowd.

The *Hausmeister* approached the pig, grabbed it around the head and thrust the dagger into its heart. The pig jumped and screamed. The man held on and twisted the knife deeper. The pig's dark eyes widened in helpless panic, and then the spirit vanished from them. The pig collapsed.

The dagger was still in the creature's heart. The *Hausmeister* was passed a large pitcher. He placed it by the dagger and withdrew. A torrent of hot blood poured in. The *Hausmeister* stirred it and passed it to one of the SS, who was smiling.

'You,' he said, pointing to an old man, 'and you and you and you,' he continued. Those selected walked forwards. 'Drink,' he ordered. And at gunpoint they drank fresh pig's blood on Yom Kippur.

Who will live and who will die? Is this a fate worse than death?

We were permitted to return to our prayers. Many felt sick and threw up. The SS shouted at us through the doors, 'God does not listen to dogs barking,' so we prayed louder.

I thought that their evil would lead to some type of instant divine retribution. Lightning would surely strike them and kill them. I prayed harder. I was disappointed. I had never felt disappointed in our God before that day.

*

In the winter of 1944, Pres Opapa sat up in his bed and said, '*Meine Kinder haben mich umgebracht*' – My children have killed me.

His pale, swollen feet stuck out from under the blanket. He let out a groan of pain and lay back down.

'What do you mean, Father?' Papa asked, his voice strained with concern.

'My David, my Shamu, their wives, their children. The burden of my worry has caused my death. *Meine Kinder haben mich umgebracht.*'

'But, father, you have received their letters,' Papa said. 'They are being worked hard, but at least the children are being looked after.'

'Rubbish! You wrote those letters. I never believed that they were genuine.'

Papa looked at his feet. It was true. He had written them.

'*Meine Kinder haben mich umgebracht,*' Pres Opapa repeated. 'I was born on *shabbat* and I will die on *shabbat*. I will not be able to speak. When I raise my hands, I want you to turn me to my right side, then I will die.'

The following Thursday, Pres Opapa took a turn for the worse.

'Eva,' Papa said, 'we need a doctor, now. Go to the public phone and call Professor Koch.'

To get to the public phone, I would have to pass through a dangerous area where all the drunken men congregated. I was scared to go alone and I looked at Papa pleadingly.

'Hurry!' he said. 'We haven't got long. Just push those drunks aside. Go!'

I did as I was told.

The doctor arrived soon after I made the call. He looked at my grandfather grimly. From the corner of the room, baby Ruth let out a whimper in my mother's arms. The doctor looked at her and said, '*Menschen kommen, Menschen gehn*' – People come and people go.

Pres Opapa raised his hands, Papa turned him onto his right side and he passed away peacefully.

Papa was a member of the *chevrah kadishah*, so he knew what he was to do. 'Come, help me,' he said. 'We must lift him off the bed and place him on the floor. Straighten him and place a serviette under his chin. That's the way. Now, hold him very still.' Papa then leaned over his father and gently closed his eyes.

Pres Opapa was taken away by horse and cart in the early hours of Friday morning. It was still dark. Papa and I rode along with the coffin. We buried him in the Jewish cemetery next to his wife. We erected tombstones for them both after the war.

Decades later, I went to visit his grave in Bratislava. I did not have to ask for directions to find his tombstone. The night of his burial was a vivid image traced in pain on the map of my childhood.

An Only Child

KLARISKÁ ULICA, BRATISLAVA, EARLY 1944

While we were living at Klariská Ulica, there were illegal raids by day and night. There were some among the Slovak population who decided to hide Jewish children. Like us, they were frightened for their lives. Yet most of the population silently collaborated with the Nazis. I remember watching thousands of young Slovak men marching down the street, heading for the front line. Their faces were grim, ready for suffering, perhaps death. Is it strange that I felt sorry for them?

The Germans had not yet occupied Hungary, so many Slovak Jews fled there with false papers. Mutti had family in various towns and cities across Hungary. Hungarian law stated that Slovak children could immigrate, provided they had family or friends in Hungary who legally adopted them. This meant that their biological parents had to abrogate all rights to them. Slovak law prohibited emigration to Hungary, though, meaning that children had to be smuggled across the border.

Mutti and Papa had a choice: they could hold on to their children, keep them close and face the fate of transportation together; or they could let them go, send them to unfamiliar places in Hungary and buy some time. With great pain, my parents chose to send their children away, except for me.

'Eva,' they explained, 'you are the oldest daughter and you do not look Jewish. You must help us here in Bratislava. You are going to stay here as our only child.'

Papa had heard of a Hungarian lady living in Bratislava who smuggled children across the border. Her name was Mrs Tafon. She was an attractive woman with sharp, gypsy-like features and a good figure.

She was unsentimental about her job; it was a high-risk venture that brought good remuneration. She assured Papa that she was good at her job, and that she would use all of her 'assets' to complete her tasks successfully.

The first to go was Marta, who was then nine years old. She left a long time before the rest of my siblings and went to live in a small town in Hungary called Sárvár, where she lived with Mutti's cousins. They taught her how to speak Hungarian and encouraged her to forget her mother tongue. It was safer that way.

Next was Kurti. He was hidden beneath a pile of hay on a cart, and dropped ten miles from the Hungarian border. There he was met by a guide, who walked with him through the forest towards the border. The route was guarded by SS officers with Alsatian dogs; if Kurti and his guide were spotted, they would have been shot on sight. Once across the border, Kurti continued to Budapest to his host family.

Mutti then travelled by train with Noemi, using false papers. She left Ruth and Renata in my care. Mutti was still breastfeeding, though, and on the train she was expressing, so she had to have Noemi suck her breasts to relieve the pain. She left Noemi with her new family and returned to Bratislava.

I was especially sad to see Noemi leave. We were very close and shared our secrets. We managed to send each other the occasional letter. Our biggest concern at that time was which of us would get her period first. In one letter Noemi told me that she had started having her period. Using our code, she wrote that 'our red auntie from America has come'.

Papa found the letter and read it. He didn't understand our code, and thought it meant that Noemi had been caught. For two weeks Papa and Mutti were crying and anxious, and I was too scared to tell them what the letter really meant. When I finally did, Papa chased me around the house, furious that we could talk of 'filthy' things at such a time.

The next to go was Judith. Fortunately, Mrs Tafon had a daughter of the same age. Judith was to cross the border using that girl's papers. Papa and I went with her to the train station to see her off. She had her blonde hair parted in the middle, tied with ribbons in sweet pigtails, and wore a little bag on her side.

Before we got to the station, Papa took her by the shoulders and said, 'Judith, you are now Mrs Tafon's daughter. You are by no means to wave at Eva and me when you leave on the train. Do you understand?'

She nodded.

Papa and I watched Judith, six years of age, board the train and take a seat. Her eyes fell on us. She did not wave at us, but at Mr Tafon, who had accompanied his wife to the station. There was wisdom in that little child.

The night before, Judith and I had sat together on our bed and devised our own secret code. Once she was in Hungary, I was to call her. I would ask, '*Nonya la non?*' and she would reply, '*Totya la tot!*' and that would mean everything was okay.

But I was never allowed to call Judith, so we never were able to use the code. I did not know it as the train departed, but that was to be the last time I ever saw her, my sweet little sister.

The last to go were Ruth and Renata, only toddlers. They were to pass as Mrs Tafon's two young sons. The day they left, a doctor came to our house and gave them both anaesthetic. Once they were asleep, I cut their beautiful hair and changed them into boys' clothing. Mrs Tafon carried the two sleeping children to the train station and took them onto the train. Mutti, Papa and I watched from a distance.

As the train raced away, I suddenly felt very lonely. For the next few months, I was the only child left in Bratislava. But I did not have time to feel sorry for myself. I was numb, and I was kept busy executing my parents' orders.

'Everything,' Papa told me, 'is now a matter of life and death.'

'I Will Be Spared'

Klariská Ulica, Bratislava, May 1944

One morning there was a knock on the door at Klariská. When I opened it, I saw two tall, blond, blue-eyed SS men, standing rigid in their high black boots. I felt a cold chill pass through my body. They walked straight past me and into the living room, took a seat and sat silently. Papa, Mutti and I watched them from a distance, not sure whether to run.

After some time, one of the men spoke. 'My name is Henek Rotstein,' he said, 'and this is my brother Victor. We have escaped Auschwitz and are in disguise, on the run. I have a girlfriend, Judith. She is sixteen. Victor has a cousin. She is nineteen. They need a place to hide.'

Henek paused for a moment. 'We understand that you have family hiding in Hungary. We thought you should know that we have just returned from Hungary, and there we saw Adolf

Eichmann. This means that Germany is about to invade Hungary, and its Jews will be deported shortly after. You should bring your children home.'

Mutti and Papa agreed to shelter the two girls, and Henek and Victor quickly left.

They were right about Hungary. After only a few weeks, Germany invaded, and Eichmann began the deportations with ruthless efficiency. Day and night my parents were on the phone to our relatives in Hungary, pleading with them to allow the children to come back to Slovakia. They refused out of fear.

Papa had no choice but to instruct Kurti, Noemi and Marta to run away from their adopted parents and meet Mrs Tafon at designated points, each different from the next, and on different dates, so as to avoid all of them being arrested at once.

We waited nervously in Bratislava for days. Noemi and Marta returned safely. Kurti, however, was late. Papa and I stood for hours next to a large arch outside our building in Klariská. Papa was stiff with fear, and with tears streaming down his face he pleaded with God to return his son.

Suddenly, I saw a tall, lanky boy, his head topped with a peasant's cap and bobbing above the crowd. We locked eyes and he came running towards us. It was Kurti. He embraced us. Papa sobbed, but his tears were now of pure joy.

*

Papa instructed Mrs Tafon to go herself and take Renata and Ruth from their family in Hungary. When Mrs Tafon arrived, the apartment was sealed and abandoned. The neighbours told her that the Germans had taken the family to a detention centre in Budapest.

Mrs Tafon could not find the children there, but she was able to seduce the guards into telling her their whereabouts. Renata and Ruth had been sent to Kistarcsa, a transit camp where Jews were held for no longer than one day. It had one train line out that went directly to Auschwitz.

Mrs Tafon rushed to the camp and found my little sisters there. How did she recognise them among all the other small children held there? Papa had told her, 'Find the child with no parents and a birthmark. She has large, black eyes. That's Ruth.'

It was just as Papa had predicted. Ruth, with her large, black eyes, was standing over Renata, who was hardly breathing, overcome by fever. Miraculously, Mrs Tafon was able to do what she had to in order to gain their release. She picked Renata up, took Ruth's hand and walked out of the camp with them.

She took Renata to a doctor, who said that the child was dying. Mrs Tafon called my father: 'If the child dies, it is not my fault. Will I still be paid?'

'Dead or alive, just bring her home,' Papa said. 'You will be paid.'

Early the next morning I was sent by taxi to meet Ruth and Renata at the border. Papa told me the night before that I was to show no emotions when I saw them. 'They will not recognise you, and you must pretend not to recognise them.'

As the taxi took me there, I kept telling myself: 'No matter what, no matter how much you want to hug and kiss them, hide your emotions.' I was scared that I would betray myself.

I spotted my little sisters from a distance. Renata was rake-thin; her blue eyes were sunken and passive. I jumped from the cab and embraced her. Next to her stood Ruth, bewildered and dirty, with scabs all over her body. I put them in the back seat of the taxi and sat between them.

The taxi driver did not start the car. He turned around slowly and looked at the three of us huddled in the back. 'Do you think I'm stupid?' he asked. 'I know these little girls are Jewish. I'm taking you to the police.'

I ignored him completely. Calmly, I said, 'Take us to the State Theatre, please.'

He looked at me suspiciously. Unlike Klariská Ulica, the State Theatre was not a Jewish area. This move changed his mind and we drove in silence to the State Theatre. From there, my little sisters and I walked back to meet our parents.

At home, Mutti and Papa started preparing Ruth and Renata to go into hiding with a new family in Slovakia. This meant they were forced to forget Hungarian and re-learn Slovakian. We could not expose the two little girls to anything that would remind them of their Jewishness. No *kiddush*, no *davening*, no *shabbat* candles.

Because they were so young, their minds were malleable enough to be shaped to different traditions and languages. We took them to a Christian lady in Bratislava who taught them to speak Slovakian, preparing them for life without their parents.

At what cost do you turn a young child away from her parents, away from her family traditions? What was happening inside their minds, inside their hearts? To this day, my little sister Renata will not identify publicly as being Jewish. She was taught at a young age not to do so.

When I think of Ruth and Renata at that time, and their wide, vacant eyes, I also think of Judith, her blonde hair in pigtails at the train station, and how she never made it back to our family. Papa ordered Mrs Tafon to go and find her, but when she did it was already too late. I think of how Judith's eyes must have looked when Mrs Tafon found her in a transit camp in Hungary, surrounded by wire fences and armed soldiers.

She was with her adopted family. The father of that family, my mother's cousin, stood tall and proud among the other prisoners. He was a highly decorated Hungarian war hero.

'I will be spared,' he told Mrs Tafon through the barbed wire. 'Judith stays with me.'

Like the rest of them, though, and like my little sister Judith, he was forced at gunpoint onto a train bound for Auschwitz, where his war medals were discarded along with spectacles, rings and children's shoes.

Our Last Goodbye

KLARISKÁ ULICA, LATE SPRING 1944

My parents were always talking quietly together, always coming and going. One evening Mutti and Papa called us all together. We sat around the kitchen table. Mutti's eyes were full of sorrow, and my Papa's face – no, his whole body – was burdened with grief.

Papa broke the silence. 'Your mother and I will do anything for the survival of this family. We have a plan. This plan will once again force us to be separated, perhaps for a long time. You will not be able to see each other or us. We know it is not easy to be apart. But you must trust us. We are doing this in order to survive.

'Listen carefully. I have found hiding places for us in Slovakia. We will all hide in pairs, and each pair will become self-sufficient and will not know the location of the others. If you are caught, you are caught as a pair, and the rest of us are spared. Kurti is to hide with Noemi; Ruth and Renata will be together; Eva will be with Marta; and Mutti and I will live with Maria Wohlschlager. I will arrange everything else.'

The next morning, Papa took Marta and me to the train station. We walked briskly and in silence. Marta and I were going to live in an apartment in Nitra that was under Maria Wohlschlager's name. We would be on our own. We had false papers attesting that we were her younger sisters. My name was to become Anca Wohlschlager, and my age sixteen; in fact, I was only twelve years old. Marta's papers had her aged ten, though neither she nor I can now remember her Aryan name.

As we walked to the station, Papa fed us information about our new identities. He made us repeat the details over and over: 'Where did you go to school? Where are your parents? Why are you living alone?'

Our train was already at the platform when we arrived. The train yard was busy. Papa pointed us in the right direction. He looked at us for a moment. *'Meine Kinder,'* he said, 'this might be our last goodbye. It is going to be difficult for you, two little girls on your own. I pray that, with God's help, you will survive. We will send you messages through Maria Wohlschlager. If there is a time when we can no longer communicate and you don't hear from us, do not come looking. Stay where you are.

'Remember: the same stars will shine over you as over Mutti and me, and those same stars also shine over Palestine.

One day we will live as free people in our own country. But until then, just look at the stars, speak to them, tell them your fears, your worries. I will also look at the stars, and I'll try my best to answer.'

The train whistled and the crowd began jostling. Papa's face suddenly became very serious. 'Most importantly, if you are ever caught, even if you are beaten or tortured, never admit to being Jewish. You are never to tell anyone that you are Jewish. You tell them the story that I just told you. You have to remember all the details. Do you understand?'

And with that, Papa let go of our hands.

Alone

Nitra, Summer 1944

Our home in Nitra was a one-room flat in a large building that had a concrete yard in the middle. Maria Wohlschlager told our neighbours that we were her sisters and that our parents had been killed during a bombing raid.

We were alone, just Marta and me. Everything frightened us. Everything was difficult. There was never enough to eat, nor was there anyone we could cry to if we were hungry, or tired, or scared. It was just Marta and me, alone in a strange town.

We couldn't speak to each other, either. Marta had only recently returned from her long period of hiding in Hungary. She had forgotten how to speak German and Slovakian, and I didn't have a word of Hungarian. We learnt how to communicate through gestures, but it was difficult and frustrating.

Marta was often overcome by anxiety. She had no way of telling me what was wrong or what she needed. She often cried loudly in her sleep.

One night I awoke to find her side of the bed empty. I looked around the room and saw her small body silhouetted in the moonlight. She was standing, naked, on the windowsill, but was still fast asleep. I was afraid that if I called out to her she might wake up with a start and fall through the window.

Instead, I tiptoed over to the window and hit her suddenly on the backs of her knees, causing her to buckle backwards into the room. She woke up in a panic. In her confusion, she started kicking and punching me furiously.

We fought often, scratching and biting each other. But mostly we kept our fear to ourselves. That small apartment in Nitra was usually dead silent.

My auntie Frida's brother lived in Nitra with his wife and four children. His family name was Haber. He owned a business right next door to where Marta and I were living. Before we arrived, though, he and his family were deported to Auschwitz, where they all perished.

The *arizátor* of Haber's business was a kind, middle-aged lady. She had tried to help Haber and his family when the Gestapo came to arrest them. Papa trusted her, so he told her about our situation. She was the only soul in Nitra who knew the truth about us. She was gentle and trustworthy. People like that were rare at this time.

Alone

She helped Papa find a hiding place for Ruth and Renata. They were to live with the coachman of Count Esterházy. The coachman lived with his family in Újlak, an hour's walk outside Nitra.

Maria Wohlschlager brought Ruth and Renata to Nitra. 'Tell the coachman that they are your cousins,' she told Marta and me, 'and that their parents were also killed in a bombing raid. Here is money for a six-month advance in return for their care.'

Maria Wohlschlager left.

*

Every Sunday in Nitra, Marta and I would go to the Catholic church for confession. We held rosary beads, learned all the prayers and crossed ourselves. We were scrutinised by a suspicious priest. It was terrifying. 'What are two little girls doing living alone here in Nitra?' he asked from behind the curtain. 'Don't you have grandparents or aunties that you could stay with?'

After church we would walk one hour to Újlak to visit Ruth and Renata. Every few miles along the path there were large wooden crucifixes stuck in the ground. We stopped at each one and crossed ourselves.

Count Esterházy's coachman and his family lived on a farm. Ruth chased chickens around the yard, and Renata chased after

Ruth. They were safe and well looked after. They had endeared themselves to the coachman's two daughters.

One Sunday, when we came to visit, Ruth was sitting in the kitchen under a hot brick stove. She had a high fever and her breathing was laboured. It was pneumonia, and the peasants thought they should keep her warm.

We asked the family to call the village doctor. Unbeknown to us, he was the only Jew in Újlak. The peasants felt that he was indispensable and had cut a deal with the Germans to spare his life.

After the war, my parents met this doctor. He told them that the day he first saw Ruth, huddled under the brick oven, he realised immediately that she was Jewish. He looked after my sisters with extra care and never said a word.

We also discovered years later that the coachman, too, knew that Ruth and Renata were Jewish. On Christmas Eve in 1944, the coachman had invited friends over to celebrate. They were drinking. They raised their glasses and said, '*Nazdravie!*' to which my sisters responded, 'Amen.'

He decided not to hand the children over to the Germans because the end of the war seemed imminent. They wanted to use the children to show the invading Russians that they were not Nazi collaborators; on the contrary, they had harboured Jewish children.

*

Alone

While Marta and I were in Nitra, I often worried that Maria Wohlschlager might one day denounce us. I lived in constant fear.

Marta and I were always hungry. We lived off meagre rations, mainly bread, and a little bit of milk if we were lucky. But we had no fresh fruit or vegetables, and absolutely no meat. We became weak and thin.

One afternoon my hunger was unbearable. I had a little bit of money left over from what Mutti and Papa had given us. I bought a tin of sardines and bread. It tasted delicious. It was a feast. That was the last of the money.

I wrote Mutti and Papa letters asking for more funds. When Maria Wohlschlager came to visit, I gave her the letters to deliver. I expected that my parents would respond immediately; we were suffering. But we heard no reply.

'Why aren't Mutti and Papa replying to my letters?' I asked Maria Wohlschlager on one of her visits. But she just kept her mouth shut. I feared that they had been caught, and that Maria could not bring herself to tell us the bad news.

I should have guessed that Maria was betraying us. She did not give Mutti and Papa my letters. Worse still, Mutti and Papa were sending us money and supplies; Maria was taking it all for herself. She stole everything, even the spare underpants they sent us. I did not learn about this until after the war.

Perhaps, in the context of what later happened, Maria Wohlschlager's betrayal does not seem so bad. But it wasn't just that she took food from our hungry mouths. She also made us feel alone. She made us feel that we would never again see our loving parents.

Interrogation

Nitra, September 1944

Our neighbours watched us closely, constantly. They were suspicious. Why should two little girls live alone? They thought the SS might find such information interesting.

One afternoon, the SS knocked on our door. There were four of them, grown men, and one Slovak collaborator from the Hlinka Guard. I stood up to speak to them while Marta stayed sitting on the bed.

The SS officers asked me questions in German. I knew that the average Slovak girl did not speak German, so I pretended I didn't understand. They motioned to the Slovak collaborator to continue the interrogation.

'Tell me, little girl, what are you doing living alone in Nitra?' he asked.

'My parents were killed in a bombing raid,' I said. 'This is my sister's apartment. Her name is Maria Wohlschlager. My name is Anca Wohlschlager.'

The questions continued for some time. I spoke consistently and with conviction. The SS were convinced, or perhaps fed up, and eventually they left.

But there was no relief. Our neighbours still spied on us, and continued relaying information to the Gestapo. I was so afraid. I didn't sleep at night. They came back to interrogate us twice more. The questions were always the same: 'What are two little girls doing alone in Nitra?'

My answers stayed consistent, to the very smallest detail, with what Papa had told me to say. We also had our fake papers and Maria Wohlschlager's testimony to validate our claims.

*

But our neighbours still watched us with almost religious devotion. They wanted us caught; they wanted us out of the building. I was as careful and as quiet as I could be, but that only made them more curious.

We made one key mistake. Learning from our mother, we always cleaned our floors, washed our clothes and bought our food on a Friday. Our neighbours always did these chores on Saturday. Once again, they had grounds for reporting us to the Gestapo.

Interrogation

This time, they sent a high-ranking officer. He wore a skull and crossbones on his hat – a *Totenkopf*, or death's head, as they called it. He was very tall and slim, with very white skin, and wore highly polished boots. His eyes were blue and handsome, but cold and intimidating. He was calm in our presence, as if he were trying to gain our confidence. He arrived unannounced in the morning and put me through a very careful cross-examination.

My story was always the same. 'My parents were killed in a bombing raid. My name is Anca Wohlschlager, sixteen years of age.' Again, I managed to convincingly argue that we were not Jewish.

As he was getting up to leave, he stopped and looked at me for a moment. 'Anca,' he said, 'I have been looking for a good nanny for quite some time. As yet I've had no luck. You seem like a capable young lady. You have been able to look after yourself and your sister alone in this apartment. How would you like a job?'

'A sixteen-year-old nanny?' I asked. 'Maybe I'm a little too young for this job, sir.'

'Nonsense. You show great maturity. You would be perfect.'

'But I have to look after my sister.'

'She could come with us,' he replied. 'I live with my family in Auschwitz. Have you heard of it? You and your sister can join us there.'

I froze. I recalled the stories of Jews being gassed in Auschwitz, of my aunties and uncles who had already been sent there.

'But, sir, if you live in Auschwitz, what are you doing in Nitra?' I asked.

'I'm here on work. We're liquidating Bratislava tomorrow. As of tomorrow, Bratislava will be *Judenfrei*.' He paused. 'But don't worry, Anca. You do not have to make a decision now. I will come back to visit you and your sister. You can tell me whether you two will be joining my family.'

As soon as the SS officer left I ran to the closest public phone. I dialled 6236, and for the first time in months I heard Papa's voice. I spoke quickly: 'As of tomorrow, Bratislava will be *Judenfrei*,' then I hung up.

After the war, Papa told me that after I hung up the phone, he took his hat and walked out of Mr Krampl's business. He walked through the streets, warning Jews to hide. And they listened. He arrived back at Klariská Ulica in the dark. At six pm the *Hausmeister* at Klariská Ulica made sure that all the Jews were inside the building. He locked the doors, then returned to his flat for dinner.

Papa and Mutti stood by their window, waiting for an opportunity to escape. Ivan, the *Hausmeister*'s son, was standing guard at the front gate. There was a call through the silence: 'Ivan, come and have your dinner.' Ivan left his post.

'Now's our chance,' Papa told Mutti. 'We must run through

the front gate and into the street. It will be busy with pedestrians. Once there, we must split up. You go right and I'll go left. Make sure nobody is following you. Make your way to Maria Wohlschlager's alone.'

'Should we pack a suitcase?' Mutti asked. 'What will we take?'

'We leave empty-handed so we don't arouse suspicion.'

That night, all the Jews at Klariská Ulica – all the Jews in Bratislava who had not found a place to hide – were pulled from their beds in the middle of the night and assembled in the Patrónka area. They were sent to Auschwitz the following day.

Gombárik

Nitra, October 1944

A few nights before Marta's tenth birthday, a Slovak man knocked on our door in Nitra. He told us that he was hiding a young Jewish couple, but that he was no longer willing to have them stay with him. 'Will you hide them?' he asked.

'We are not Jewish,' I responded. 'Why would you ask us?'

'They told me you are Jewish. They know you from Bratislava.' I was horrified that this Jewish couple had told their hosts we were Jewish. It put us at great risk. Nevertheless, we agreed and the young Jewish couple moved in.

They stayed with us for a few nights, and then left on the morning of Marta's birthday. They had found somewhere new to hide.

Marta and I went out for the first time in days. By now we were again able to communicate. Marta had remembered some of her Slovakian and German, while I had picked up a bit of Hungarian.

We walked down to the street stall to collect our food rations. The sun was out. The street was busy with people shopping and chatting.

I heard the fall of boots and looked up to see twenty-five soldiers marching in a line, machine guns on their shoulders. They were led by a short man with an Alsatian on a leash. He stopped outside the building where Marta and I lived. My eyes widened. I tried to look unconcerned, not wanting to arouse suspicion. I heard the short man shout an order. The twenty-five soldiers marched into our building.

I suddenly realised that they were coming for us. They might have caught the Jewish couple, I thought, or maybe their host family had told the authorities the truth about us. 'Run to the Habers' shop and hide,' I whispered to Marta.

The shopkeeper saw her walking away. 'Just go home,' he shouted. 'They will catch you anyway.'

I pretended not to hear him and walked off in the opposite direction. The people in the street heard the shopkeeper and started to shout at me, all at once: 'Go home. There is no escape.' They surrounded me, a mob of faceless adults. They herded me into our building and upstairs to the apartment. The short man was waiting.

*

The soldiers stood in a circle, and I was thrown into the middle. There stood the short man with the Alsatian. He was bald, plump and had small, cruel eyes. He stared at me for a long time. His name was Gombárik, and he was head of the Hlinka Guard.

I could hear Marta shouting in the stairwell. The door opened and she was thrown into the room by a mob of Slovak civilians. The *arizátor* at the Habers' business had not been able to hide her; the mob had followed Marta there.

One of the soldiers picked Marta up and threw her down on the bed. I looked at her and saw terror in her eyes. I wanted to do something to help. What could I do?

No one said a word. Marta was crying and the soldiers were shuffling their feet. I looked at the floor. Gombárik took a few steps towards me. 'I'm here to ask you a few questions, little girl,' he said.

He gave the Alsatian's leash to one of the soldiers, pulled a pair of silver knuckle-dusters from his pocket and slipped them on his hands.

'What's your name?' he asked.

'My name is Anca Wohlschlager.'

He reached out a hand, took hold of my neck and squeezed. Without saying a word, he brought his other fist down into my right temple with the silver tip of his knuckle-duster. My vision went white and I felt like I was about to throw up.

'I know you are Jewish,' he continued. 'Tell me your name or there will be more of this, a lot more.'

Above: Pres Opapa and Pres Omama in the early 1900s.

Below left: My mother's father, Leopold Kerpel.

Below right: The family textiles business, The Brothers Weiss, on Michalská Brána, Bratislava.

Above: The wedding of my parents, Eugene and Margaret Weiss, in 1929.

Top left: My cousins, David and Frida's children, Gabriel, Rutti, Miriam and Ernst.

Top right: My beautiful cousin Miriam.

Above: Kurti, me, Noemi and Marta in costume.

Left: Shamu and Dina's children, my cousins Ephraim, Moshe, Yitl and Gitl.

Above: With some staff members and other children at Ľubochňa in the Tatra Mountains. Our nanny Maria Wohlschlager is on the far right in the back row. Kurti is in the centre of the front row, and to his left are Marta, me and Noemi.

Below: My cousins and me with Maria Wohlschlager and Auntie Aranka, my mother's sister. I am standing on the right, and baby Judith is sitting on Maria Wohlschlager's knee.

Above: The last photo of me before leaving for Nitra, with Ruth and Renata. I was twelve years old.

Left: My little sister Judith at the train station in Bratislava, leaving for Hungary. It was the last time I saw her.

Above: The star worn by my father.

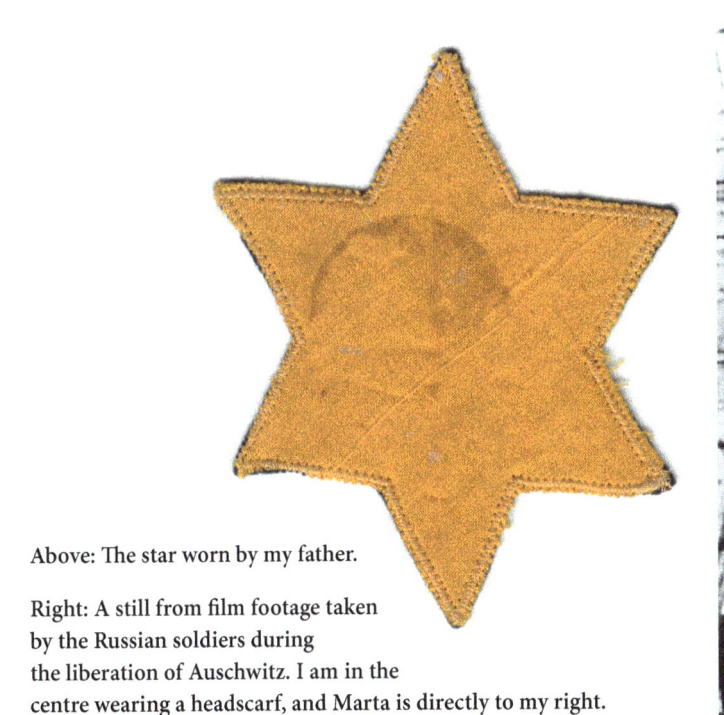

Right: A still from film footage taken by the Russian soldiers during the liberation of Auschwitz. I am in the centre wearing a headscarf, and Marta is directly to my right.

Below right: After the war in Bratislava. Mutti, me and Noemi are in the back row, with Rosanna, Renata, Hannah and Ruth in the front.

Below: Revisiting Auschwitz on the sixtieth anniversary of liberation with other child survivors, recreating the widely seen image at the top right.

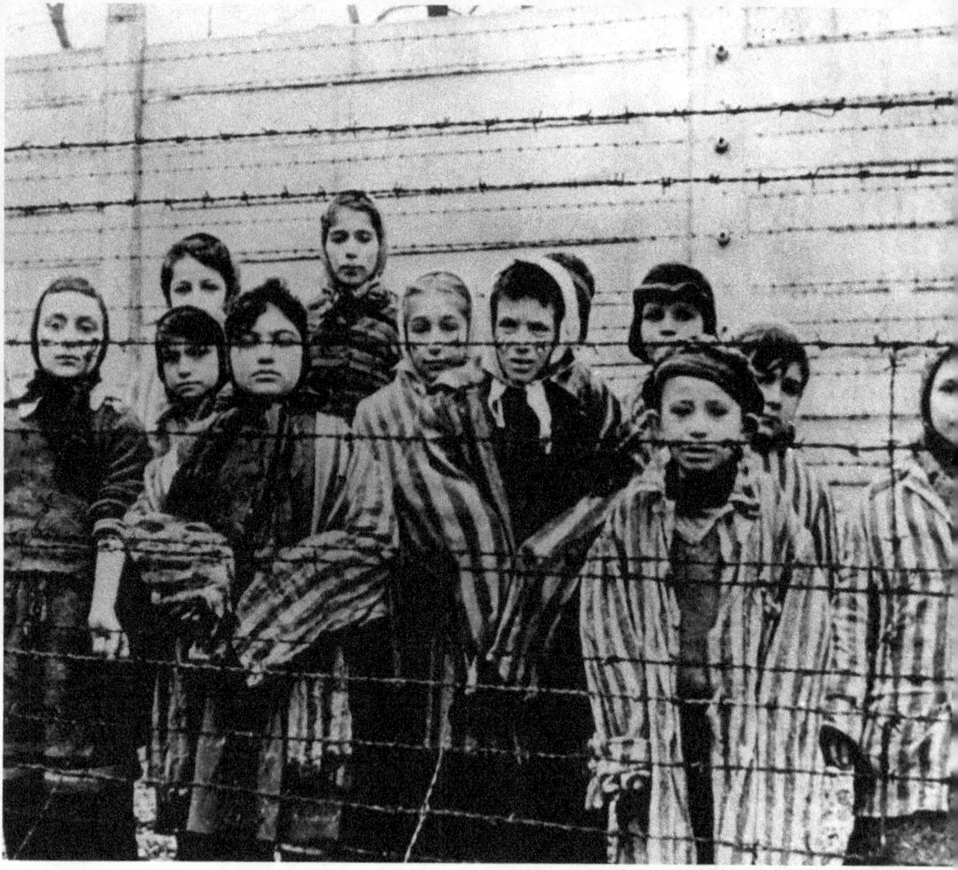

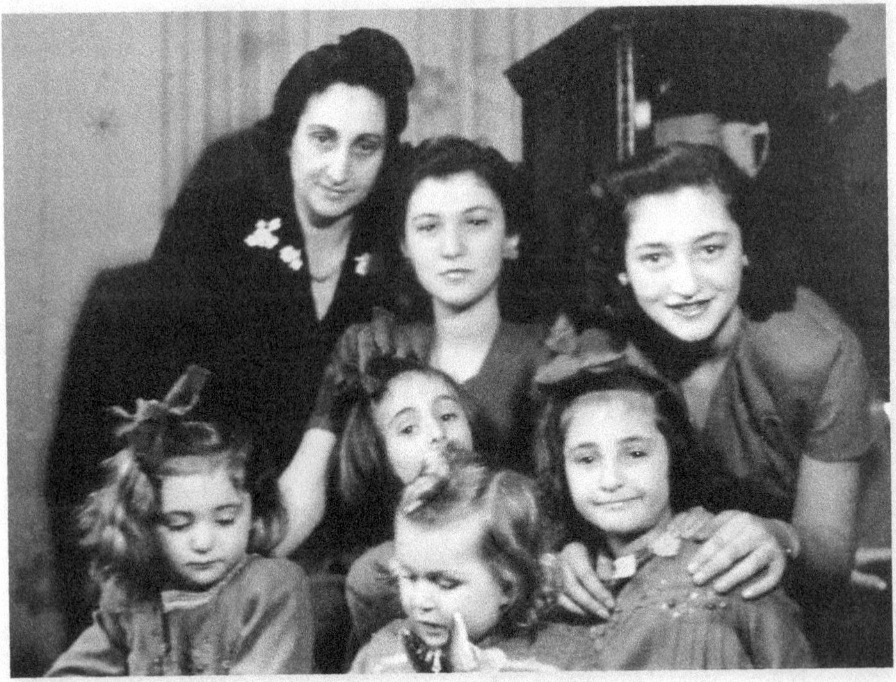

Left: My son Malcolm's bar mitzvah in Australia. From left: Edwin, Sharona, Daniel, Ben, Aviva, me and Malcolm.

Below: The family together in Australia.

Below: My husband, Ben Slonim, with the Weiss family *sefer Torah* at Mizrachi Synagogue, Melbourne.

Below: Ben and me on my seventieth birthday.

I clenched my fist and closed my eyes. I was petrified. I felt helpless. Suddenly, I had a vision of Papa. He was insisting on something, insisting over and over: 'Never admit to being Jewish. It is your own death sentence.'

Gombárik's grip around my neck tightened, and I felt another blow to my temple. I opened my eyes wide and shouted, 'My name is Anca Wohlschlager! Our parents died in a bombing raid in Bratislava. Our sister's name is Maria Wohlschlager, and she comes to visit us frequently. We can prove it. We are not Jewish.'

Gombárik kept asking my name and why we were by ourselves in Nitra. I gave the answers that Papa had told us to give, but Gombárik would not relent. He took the Alsatian back from the soldier and positioned it in front of me, its teeth bared, then let go of the leash. I jumped up and climbed the wardrobe next to the bed. The dog barked furiously below me. Twenty-five soldiers were laughing and pointing.

Gombárik took the leash and passed it back to the soldier. He walked over to the wardrobe. 'Is there anything you'd like to tell me?' he asked. 'Or do you want me to take this a little further?'

I could hear Marta crying below. 'I swear to you, I'm telling you the truth!'

Gombárik grabbed my arm and wrenched me from the wardrobe to the floor. 'Stand up!' he shouted. 'Now, take off your skirt.'

I did.

'And now take off your underpants.'

The soldiers started to chuckle again. I felt very humiliated.

'Now, bend over this chair.'

I bent over the wooden chair and stared at the floor, unsure what was going to happen. I felt a sharp pain on the back of my legs and buttocks. Gombárik was beating me with a leather baton. As he continued, the soldiers boisterously counted along with him: 'Forty-eight . . . forty-nine . . . fifty . . .'

'Would you like to tell me your name or would you like this to continue?'

With my face to the ground, I pleaded with him: 'I swear, everything I said is the truth! I can't tell you anything more!' There was a vision of Papa in front of my eyes, urging me to stay strong. I was never going to tell.

Gombárik pushed me up against a wall and leaned his full weight onto my torso. He slid his hand underneath my shirt and onto my stomach. I felt him grab my flesh and twist. I writhed in pain. Then his hand went higher up to my breasts. He pinched and twisted them. The pain was indescribable. I felt that I could not hold out much longer. He released me and I slumped to the floor.

Next, Gombárik reached into his breast pocket and pulled out a revolver. 'Soldiers, close the windows,' he said, and slowly he attached a silencer to the barrel. Marta was whimpering, even though she couldn't understand what he was saying. 'I'm going to ask you one more time. Is there anything you want to tell me? Your name, perhaps?'

I closed my eyes. *I should tell him the truth*, I thought, *and then somehow we'll be spared. Maybe he'll have pity on us?* I felt Gombárik's revolver press against my temple. Papa was with me at this moment, and I heard his voice of reason: 'If you tell him you are Jewish, you are dead anyway.' I listened. I didn't say a word.

Marta screamed. The soldiers lifted her off the bed and threw her down the stairs. Gombárik withdrew his revolver, then the soldiers picked me up and threw me down after Marta. We scrambled up and ran out to the street.

The soldiers were throwing all of our possessions, all the textiles Papa had given Maria Wohlschlager in return for hiding us, out of the window and down to the street below. Our neighbours were smiling, laughing and cheering. At that moment, I swore that I would never forgive them.

*

Among the crowd was a young German girl called Grete. I had made friends with her during the weeks previous. Her father was the *Obersturmführer* in Nitra; if we were ever arrested, I hoped he might be able to help us. We made eye contact and Grete came running towards me. 'Where are they taking you, Anca?' she cried.

'They think I'm Jewish,' I said. 'They're taking us away. Maybe your father could vouch for us?'

'Papa is out of town,' she said, and my heart sank. 'Is there anything I can do?'

I thought about my parents. I wanted to warn them not to try to reach us, and to tell Maria Wohlschlager to stay in Bratislava. I leaned forward and whispered into Grete's ear: 'You must call the number 4393 from a public phone. Tell whoever answers the phone that the goods have all been taken.'

As I finished my sentence, a soldier lifted me around the waist. Marta and I were thrown onto a truck and transported to the local detention centre.

Grete did exactly as I asked of her and called Maria Wohlschlager's house. Papa answered the phone. When he heard Grete say, 'All the goods have been taken,' he knew that Marta and I had been arrested. He and Mutti left for a new hiding place without saying a word to Maria Wohlschlager.

Their new hiding place was with a German man called Misbacher. He was married to a wealthy countess, although he was twenty years her junior. She was a staunch Catholic and an anti-Semite. But she was also a serious alcoholic. Misbacher was able to hide Mutti and Papa in her large apartment right under her nose without her realising. Papa ran Misbacher's business in return.

*

Gombárik

After the war, my sister Noemi told us that on the very same day we were taken – Marta's tenth birthday – she had called Mutti and Papa at Maria Wohlschlager's from a milk bar, only half an hour after Grete's call. A man had answered in German – it was the Gestapo. On Gombárik's orders, they had gone to search Maria Wohlschlager's house, suspecting that she was harbouring more Jews there.

The German shouted over the phone: 'Who is this? Tell me where you're hiding!'

Noemi dropped the receiver and ran out of the milk bar, back to her hiding place with Kurti.

For the rest of the war, Kurti and Noemi believed that Mutti and Papa had been caught. Lives were saved and lives were lost in mere minutes.

Torture

Nitra Detention Centre, October 1944

Marta and I were taken to the detention centre in Nitra. It was really just a large cellar. Around a hundred Jewish prisoners were held there. Along the walls were bare wooden shelves, three tiers high and about a foot wide. That was where we were to sleep.

People at the detention centre didn't talk much, and families generally kept to themselves. I knew only one: Mr and Mrs Krasnansky, and their son Ivan. They had another son who was only a toddler.

Even though Ivan was two years younger than me, we had been good friends back in Bratislava. When the first anti-Jewish laws came in and we were no longer allowed to play in the public parks, we would walk into the hills around the city. It was springtime and the fields were covered in poppies. We would eat them and forget our troubles.

Ivan's father was a brilliant man. He was the architect for Slovakia's president, Josef Tiso. I once overheard him saying to the other inmates, 'Any day now I will be given my presidential pardon.' He gave away his meagre food rations, looking on the rest of us as if we were the condemned.

I would later see him among the crowd at Auschwitz. By that time there was a deep void in his eyes. Ivan would be the only surviving Krasnansky.

*

There was hardly anything to eat at the detention camp. People were always talking about food, and guarded what they got like it was sacred property. Only those deemed fit for work were given any rations. My job was to sort confiscated Jewish goods, but Marta was not given any work. We shared my rations and both grew skinnier.

Torture became a part of my daily routine, my morning ritual, like breakfast or coffee for most people. The sound of boots on concrete was my alarm clock. Every morning at four am, I was taken from my wooden shelf and led by soldiers to Gombárik's chambers for interrogation. There were others in the detention camp who were also questioned and tortured in this way. Gombárik was obsessed with getting information about the remaining Jews hiding in Slovakia.

'What is your name?' he would ask every day.

'My name is Anca Wohlschlager.'

'Little girl,' he would continue, 'do you want me to send you to be turned into canned meat?'

These days, I wear earplugs to sleep. Nevertheless, every morning at four, I am woken up by the sound of boots on concrete. I jump out of bed, check the door and try to go back to sleep.

*

One morning I was sorting through confiscated goods when a plump, middle-aged woman with blonde hair came and stood next to me. I had not seen her before and was immediately suspicious. It was common for the Gestapo to use Jews to spy on other Jews. They would be offered freedom in return for information.

'Do you know what this is?' she asked me, holding up a *tallit*.

'I think it's just a blanket, isn't it?' I replied, looking down at my work.

'And what about this? What do you think this is? I'm not quite sure . . .'

I looked up and saw that the woman was holding a Jewish prayer book. 'I believe that's a Bible,' I said.

'Now, how would an average Catholic girl like you be able to recognise a Bible written in another language?' she asked.

Torture

I was scared. I couldn't think of an excuse. I heard the words '*Werden wir leben, werden wir sehn*' coming from my mouth, almost involuntarily: If we will live, then we will see.

'Aha!' the lady cried. 'That is a Jewish proverb, isn't it?'

In the workshop was a lanky young man named Simon. Probably around eighteen years old, he had gentle, handsome eyes. He was eavesdropping on the interrogation. Simon picked up a box of goods and walked towards the door. As he passed me, he leaned forward and whispered, 'Don't say another word. She has nothing on you.' I did as he instructed and kept my mouth shut.

The next morning I was woken by the sound of boots on concrete. This time, I was not taken to Gombárik's chambers. All of us prisoners were dragged out of our concrete cellar and ordered to the yard. Standing alone, against a brick wall, was Simon. All the colour drained from his face. We were lined up in a row facing him.

Gombárik came forward and stood in front of the crowd. 'This morning you will witness the execution by gunshot of two Jews,' he announced.

He cocked his rifle, took aim and shot Simon in the head. His young body collapsed.

I began trembling. Was this my fault? I was sure I was to be the next executed.

From the far side of the yard I heard a woman sobbing. She was holding her three-year-old daughter in her arms, and limping between two SS officers as they positioned her on the wall next to Simon's body. One of the SS soldiers grabbed the child from the woman's arms and dropped her on the ground. The toddler clung to her mother's leg. She was, as three-year-olds are, perfectly innocent.

Gombárik continued speaking: 'This Jew tried to escape last night. She jumped from the window with her child. She broke her leg. Let this be a warning to you all.'

He raised his rifle, took aim and shot the woman in the head. She dropped dead next to her child. The toddler looked down at her mother and started to cry.

Gombárik let another few moments go by. The courtyard was silent except for the toddler's whimpers. We waited. Gombárik took aim a third time and let the child join her mother. Three bodies lay in front of the wall, with one hundred pairs of eyes staring at them.

Shortly after the war ended, I was summoned to Nitra to testify as a witness in Gombárik's trial for war crimes. I stayed in a pub near the courthouse, and I could hear Slovak soldiers drinking all night. I was very frightened.

During the trial I gave testimony about everything I saw Gombárik do. I told of how he tortured me, and how he shot Simon and the mother and child. In the gallery sat all of Gombárik's former henchmen, now free citizens. They smirked and jeered during my testimony.

Gombárik denied everything. He looked at the judge and

said, with mock sincerity, 'I would never lay a finger on a child. Never.'

I think the judge in this trial was Jewish. During the proceedings he examined me very carefully, very rigorously. He continuously asked about Simon's death, how he was shot and why he was shot.

Gombárik was found guilty and condemned to death. I was later told that Simon was the judge's son.

Caught

Nitra Detention Centre, October 1944

After just over two weeks at Nitra, Marta and I were summoned to a tribunal hearing. We were escorted to the soldiers' barracks at the far end of the detention centre.

At the end of the barracks I could see a large table with around eight men sitting on one side, facing us. As we walked closer I could make out the man sitting in the middle: Gombárik, his eyes squinted in a cynical smile.

Gombárik stood up. 'Good morning, girls,' he said mockingly. 'I have some information that you two might find interesting. Your sister, this Maria Wohlschlager, we visited her in her apartment in Bratislava. We asked her a few questions about her little sisters living in Nitra.'

I shuddered.

Caught

'Would you like to know what your older sister said about you? I'm going to give you one more chance. Little girl, what is your name?'

I looked Gombárik in the eye. 'My name is Anca Wohlschlager.'

Gombárik brought his fist down on the table with great force, sending an echo through the barracks. 'Liar!' he screamed. 'You are Eva Weiss, thirteen years old. And she is your little sister Marta. She just turned ten. You are two Jewish girls, and you are going to be sent far away.'

The next morning Gombárik and his men escorted us to the train station. Jews were being herded into a train, one after the other. All were bound for Sered', a transit camp on the way to Auschwitz.

At the entrance to the train station was a man I recognised. I could tell by the way he was looking at me that he recognised me too. It was my friend Grete's father. He was back from Germany and, on Grete's request, had come looking for us. I waved frantically to him. He came running over and started talking to Gombárik, gesturing with his hands.

Gombárik watched him, smirking. 'I'm sorry, sir, but you are mistaken,' he said. 'These two girls are Jewish. They go by the name of Weiss. They had you fooled. But not to worry, they will be dealt with along with the rest.'

Gombárik took me with one arm and Marta with the other, and personally walked us towards the train. He threw Marta inside, then drew me close to his face. 'Goodbye, my Christian friend, Anca Wohlschlager, sixteen years old,' he said. 'And goodbye, my Jewish friend, Eva Weiss, thirteen years old. We will never see each other again.'

Devoid of strength and hope, deprived, humiliated and brutalised, my body and soul destroyed, I felt I had lost my resolve to fight for my life.

'Not unless I turn up in one of your cans of meat,' I replied, and boarded the train.

Orphaned, All of Us

On the Train to Sereď, late October 1944

The train was crowded and there was no room to sit. Families huddled together and infants cried. I stood next to Marta in silence and scanned the carriage for familiar faces.

My eyes settled on a young Slovak soldier who had sympathetic eyes. I put my hand in my jacket pocket and felt a gold pen that I had stolen from the confiscated goods pile at the detention camp in Nitra. I held the pen firmly in one hand and Marta's hand in the other, and pushed my way through the crowd towards the young soldier.

When we reached him, I whispered: 'If I give you this gold pen, will you shoot at us if we jump from the train?'

He took the pen from my hand, looked at me and nodded. 'I will have to shoot at you,' he said, 'but I'll do my best to miss.'

'What about the other guards?' I asked. 'Will they shoot?'

'I cannot control their aim. You will have to try your luck. The odds are against you.'

The soldier pocketed the gold pen, my last possession, and we continued on the train to the transit camp in Sered'.

*

After many hours the train came to a halt and the door slid open. I saw people everywhere, all standing in lines, being herded in different directions. A faceless voice was shouting orders in German over a loudspeaker. The soldiers ordered us off the train.

I noticed one SS man who looked as if he was overseeing the operation. It was Alois Brunner, an assistant of Eichmann; he would later seek refuge from prosecution in Syria. I broke line in order to speak with him.

'Excuse me, sir,' I said in my best German. 'There has been a terrible mistake. You see, my sister and I, we are not Jewish. We are Catholic. We have been wrongly arrested, and if you just give me a few minutes I can prove it to you.'

He looked at me with cold eyes and, without hesitating, kicked me to the ground and walked away.

There was a call over a loudspeaker: 'Attention: experienced or professional hand-knitters, please make yourselves known. Those who qualify will be held back from deportation.'

I did not know how to knit as much as a scarf. Nevertheless, I thought of a story on the spot and made myself known. The lady in charge was a short Jewish woman.

'I am from a poor family,' I began. 'Mother taught me how to knit at a young age to support the family. I am very experienced. But I will only stay and help if my little sister can stay with me.'

I told my story with such conviction that the woman agreed. She handed me an unfinished jumper that was being knitted for an SS woman. It was pink angora wool with a complex black pattern across the neckline. 'Finish this,' she ordered, and gave me a needle and a ball of yarn.

I pretended to study the design and the wool until I heard the shrill whistle of the train departing for Auschwitz. I started 'knitting' and the jumper began to unravel; the stitches ran from my needle like they were being chased. After about an hour the overseer inspected my work. I was beaten for my deception.

Marta and I were ordered into a large room that was filled with prisoners awaiting deportation. There was no space to lie down, so we remained standing all night.

*

It was still dark when the SS men marched us out of the building and onto the waiting cattle train. We piled on: men, women, children, the sick and elderly, infants in their mothers' arms.

I heard the same shrill whistle, we were bolted in, and then we departed.

A day passed by in sheer terror. We had no food and no water. People began to collapse; those who did rarely managed to stand up again.

The carriage was packed beyond capacity. It was dark and there was little air. In the middle of the carriage was a small bucket for excreta. But it was too crowded for anyone to move, so those who were desperate did what they had to on the floor.

That night we made a brief stop. We started screaming, 'Water, we need water!' But our screams fell dead in the night.

Opposite me, a young mother held her baby girl. It cried from hunger. After two days without food or water, the mother was no longer able to breastfeed. The baby screamed but the mother could do nothing but stroke its face tenderly. The baby cried ceaselessly.

As I watched the mother caress her baby, I felt a longing to be in my parents' arms. Marta and I were the only children I could see on the train without their parents. I felt like an orphan. *If Mutti and Papa were here, everything would be okay,* I thought to myself. *They would look after me, hold me close.* I hoped that God would offer me protection, and I prayed silently for a miracle. I was sure that God would grant us a reprieve.

On our third day on the train, the baby girl stopped crying. I looked across at the mother and saw a lifeless infant in her arms. The young mother continued to stroke the little face tenderly, and occasionally whispered a few words into the baby's ear.

My prayers weren't answered. I felt as if no one was watching over us. We were alone, abandoned, orphaned, all of us. During that long and terrible journey, my faith began to sway to and fro, and it has done so for the rest of my life.

I will never presume to understand the workings of God, but to question them and to bemoan them is not a sin. I realise now that by questioning God, I was preserving the relevance of my faith. I have questioned, suffered disappointments, often rebelled and despaired, but I have never shut down my dialogue with God. God was never dead – there was never any doubt in my mind that some of us would survive, or that those who did would continue that difficult, painful dialogue between the Jewish people and their God.

I saw that lifeless baby in her mother's arms, and even though I accused God for letting it happen, I brokered a deal. *If I survive*, I prayed, *I will give birth to many more Jewish children.*

*

The journey seemed endless. The elderly and the sick died next to their families. A few more days and we, too, would have perished. But suddenly the train stopped. Above the stench of human excrement, we could smell something different, something even more putrid.

One of the men standing near us picked Marta up and held her to the barred window. 'What can you see, little girl? Tell us what you see.'

'I can see big chimneys,' Marta replied, 'and I can see lots of smoke.'

Our First Day

Auschwitz-Birkenau, 3 November 1944

The doors were flung open. The snow was blinding. German soldiers boarded the train, shouting orders: 'Women with infants, children under sixteen and old people to the right; young men and women without children to the left.' We obeyed.

Marta and I walked towards the right. A young man started tugging at my arm. 'This is selection,' he said. 'You look old enough – come with us!'

I looked at Marta, confused.

'Go with them,' she said. 'Go with the living. I am not scared to die alone. Just remember this date, and tell Papa to say *kaddish* for me.'

I felt the young man tug again at my arm. I succumbed and inched to the left, towards the living. But then I felt another tug coming from the opposite direction, this time on my skirt. I looked down and saw Marta gripping to my garment.

'Eva, I'm too scared to die on my own.'

Just a few days earlier, even letting Marta out of my sight had been unthinkable to me. And now I was willing to leave her amid the chimneys and smoke? I felt very guilty.

I pulled my arm away from the young man and took Marta's instead. 'We will never be separated again,' I told her. 'I promise.'

*

Dogs barked and SS men shouted, *'Raus, raus!'* Marta and I were pushed to the right, and our crowd was ordered to form lines of five. We started marching.

I will never forget that first march through Birkenau. I saw prisoners standing behind electric wire, their heads shaven, with filthy rags hanging off their bones. I will never forget their eyes, overgrown in their emaciated heads – they were mad-looking, desperate, two great voids scanning the newly arrived for relatives.

I wanted to survive, yes. I was desperate to remain with the living. But to live like this? To become like them? To me, they did not look human. During that march, I prayed to God. I did not ask for survival. No. My prayer was: *Please, God, let me keep my humanity. Do not turn me into one of them.*

Our First Day

As we marched through the camp, we had no idea if we were going to live or die. Whispers went through the lines that we were to be spared. We marched slowly on, to an unknown destination.

We crossed a small bridge with no balustrades, flanked by men with guns. Open sewage flowed beneath us. One of the SS men kicked Marta off the bridge. She screamed and thrashed frantically in the stream of excrement. She would have drowned if not for a brave young man who jumped in after her and pulled her out. The soldiers whooped and laughed.

Eventually, we stopped outside a large barracks. We were ordered to enter. It was long, narrow and dark, with wooden slats for beds. In the middle of the barracks was a stout man standing on a chair. He was the *Blockälteste* of the *Familienlager*.

'Every beginning has its end,' he shouted. 'One word, one step out of line, and you are dead.' He then ordered us back outside.

I will never forget that first day. There are moments that, perhaps, I wish I could forget. Back outside in the yard, I saw that a gallows had been erected. We were lined up in front of it. Two SS men led a young girl to the gallows. She looked no older than me. They placed a noose around her neck and I began to sob uncontrollably.

'Don't cry,' a *kapo* standing next to me whispered. 'She is lucky. She will not feel a thing. Her friends managed to find sedatives to drug her beforehand. Her suffering is over.'

I remember seeing the girl hanging from the gallows. Her suffering was not over, I knew. It lives on, and it repeats endlessly in my memory.

Night fell, and we were ordered back into our barracks. Marta was still wet from the sewage, and there was no water with which to wash. She was hysterical and cold.

Our first meal arrived. It was a cup of weak coffee. Everyone in the barracks donated their ration to wash Marta. Then some of the men sat around a makeshift table and talked seriously, trying to come to terms with what was happening. They made a makeshift ouija board and tried to speak to the dead. We were all scared.

The *Familienlager*

Auschwitz-Birkenau, November 1944

The morning after we arrived in Birkenau we were lined up outside our barracks. The *Blockälteste* walked in front of us, staring. He was short and stout, and had a booming voice. He pointed at me. 'You will be my *stubova*, my helper.'

I was taken to his room at the front right of the barracks. In it was a cooking stove, a bed and a table. My duties were simple enough. I had to cook his food and clean his room. I took my time. His room was warm from the stove.

I thought it was a good idea to take my shoes off and leave them with Marta. I wanted to prevent them from wearing out. Shoes, an inmate had whispered to me, were more valuable than food.

When I finished my chores I went looking for Marta. She was standing in one of the corners of the barracks.

'Where are my shoes?' I asked.

'I'm sorry, Eva.'

'What did you do with them?'

Poor Marta looked so frightened. 'There was a woman on the other side of the electric fence who told me that she would give me a piece of bread if I threw over your shoes,' she said. 'I was so hungry, Eva. I'm so sorry.'

'Where's the bread, then?' I asked

Marta looked at the floor. 'I threw the shoes over first. She told me that we were both going to die anyway. She didn't give me the bread.'

This is how Marta and I learnt about life in Birkenau.

*

Over the next few days I continued to do chores for the *Blockälteste*. Generally, he left me alone. One day I was boiling water on the stove when he stormed into his small room, screaming. He took off his cap and swiped the cooking pots off the stove. The hot water spilled on my left arm and burnt it.

'Do you think I chose you as my helper because you are pretty?' he yelled.

I was silent.

'No! I chose you because you look like my daughter who was gassed.'

He grabbed me by the arm and dragged me to the latrine.

His sorrow, his despair had transformed into a furious rage, and he let it out on me. He pushed my head into the latrine. I begged him to stop. He held me there until I threw up.

'Get up and go back to your barracks,' he shouted.

He was killed after liberation by survivors.

A27201

Auschwitz-Birkenau, November 1944

One morning we were woken up earlier than usual, when it was still dark. It was around four am. We were ordered into the yard to be counted; this was called *tzel apel*. We were given a cup of weak coffee and a slice of bread for breakfast. Then we were marched to a different barracks for tattooing. We did not know what this meant, and we were afraid that it was preparation for the gas chambers.

When it was my turn, I held out my left arm, trembling. The man giving the tattoos was a Jewish inmate. He held my burnt arm gently. 'Those who are tattooed have been chosen to live,' he said softly.

I was momentarily reassured by this kind man. But then suddenly I realised that I was no longer the girl I had been just a day before. I was no longer Eva Weiss, thirteen years of age. I was not even Anca Wohlschlager, sixteen years of age. I was A27201.

Once we had all been tattooed, we were commanded to line up in fives and march, so we did. We marched past a huge concrete pit. Behind it, at some distance down the path, there were birch trees swaying in the wind.

After the war, I learnt that this pit was my sister Judith's grave. Judith had tried to escape the night her adopted family was arrested in Hungary. She jumped out of the window in her room and into the neighbours' yard. She had put sugar cubes in her pocket to appease their dogs. Unfortunately, the dogs barked and she was caught. On arriving at Auschwitz, she was put in a tipping truck with hundreds of other little children, and thrown alive into this concrete pit, at the bottom of which was a fire.

I walked past her grave without a second glance. If I had known then that this was her final resting place, I would have whispered *kaddish* for her, my little sister. But beyond the concrete pit the birch trees swayed, as if performing an eternal *kaddish* for Judith and the rest of those children.

*

We marched on, towards what we were told was the 'sauna'. It was no sauna. It was a large concrete chamber where, at gunpoint, we had to strip. From the corner of my eye I saw my old teacher, Laura-neni, whom I revered and respected, now naked and quivering under the barrel of a gun.

Then we were pushed into another room, naked and cold. There, they shaved off all of our hair. We were completely robbed of our dignity. We were given a towel and a piece of soap. They told us that the soap was made from human fat.

We were pushed into a small concrete chamber which had showerheads hanging from the roof. Some of the older prisoners started shouting, 'We will be gassed!' and were forced in. The door was bolted shut. The room filled with screams and moans. Cold water drenched us from above.

When the water was shut off, the back door of the chamber opened. We were pushed out and, still naked, were ordered to bow our heads. As we shivered in the cold, our newly shaven heads were doused with petrol. It was called disinfection.

The guards threw us some clothes. Mine were disgusting. The shirt was missing a sleeve and the underpants had been soiled. Somehow, in the rush, Marta stole an extra set of clean garments, which she put one on top of the other, saving one for me.

At the end of that day I no longer felt like I knew who I was.

Toddlers' Barracks

Auschwitz-Birkenau, November 1944

Marta and I were taken to the toddlers' barracks, a big bare shed that looked just like the others. We were the oldest, except for another girl called Bushi, who was around my age. We were put in charge of about seventy young children, many under the age of three. There was nothing to feed them.

At night we heard the mothers of the children banging on the door of our barracks, screaming for their children. Then we saw the *Blockälteste* from the barracks where the mothers were housed pulling them away. The image of those children, half-asleep and reaching for their mothers, still haunts me. But what was worse were the sounds, the shrill cries of the desperate mothers, the piercing shrieks of their children. To this day, the sound of a baby crying takes me back to that time, and I shudder.

We spent three nights without food or milk in the toddlers' barracks. The babies would cry incessantly; they would stop only when approaching death.

On the fourth morning, the door was flung open and a large can of milk was thrown in. As I went to retrieve it, a *kapo*, a woman I recognised from Bratislava, came running and tried to snatch it. Bushi and I fought her for the milk, but she hit us repeatedly until we gave in.

She looked me in the eyes, clutching the can of milk there in the barracks full of hungry babies and toddlers. 'You will all die anyway,' she said. 'I deserve this milk. I've been here for years.'

Mengele

Twins' Barracks, Auschwitz-Birkenau, November–December 1944

We had all heard about Dr Josef Mengele, who was known for having an interest in twins. One morning Marta and I were ordered to a new barracks on the other side of the camp, close to the hospital. It was basically the same as the other barracks – dark, dirty, crowded – except that those inside were pregnant women, twins and people with physical disabilities or genetic quirks. Apparently, Dr Mengele had been watching Marta and me. He mistakenly took us for twins. To be a twin at Auschwitz meant to stay alive, but at a cost.

Among those in our new barracks was a family of circus performers. They were Hungarian. Before the war, they had travelled from town to town doing their act. There were nine of them, and eight were dwarves. Mengele was fascinated by them.

Most of us in that barracks were children. How we suffered there. Alone, without our parents, in the middle of a waking hell.

Mengele's presence hung over us. He would stroll past our bunks and look at us. His gaze was almost paternal, perversely caring, but it was cold. It said: *You are my toys, and I will decide what happens to you, and when. And I will play with you until you are of no more use to me.*

What was more, we were ordered to play cruel, inhuman games. One was 'The Farmer Wants a Wife'. We would stand in a circle, and Mengele would walk around us until he chose the Farmer. The Farmer went into the middle of the circle.

'Now, Farmer, you must choose a wife,' Mengele would say, as if he were a schoolteacher.

Whomever the Farmer chose was taken away for medical experiments, and seldom returned. Mengele made us choose.

I often wondered what happened to the Farmer's wife. One day, on my way back from emptying the barracks' bucket of excrement in the sewer, I saw the door of a room left slightly ajar.

I tiptoed into the room. It was filled with the dismembered body parts of the children who had left our barracks. Bodies lying like broken dolls. I saw the torso of a boy who had been in our transport from Sered'. His arms and legs were stacked next to him in a pile.

I saw this with the eyes of a thirteen-year-old. I was a child.

*

There was a boy in our barracks who never said a word. All day, he would sit on the brick oven and sway back and forth, back and forth. He left his spot only at four in the morning, when we were chased out for roll call and breakfast – black coffee, one slice of bread – and then again at four in the afternoon, also for roll call and nightly rations – a watery liquid called soup and a slice of bread. But at all other times, he would sit and sway, back and forth, back and forth.

Who was this boy? No one knew his name. He didn't speak. Perhaps he was unable to talk because of what he had seen. Perhaps he was simply unable to open his mouth.

I stared at him and imagined him *davening*, studying our sacred texts with long *payot* in the *cheder*, surrounded by other young Jewish boys. And then I would see him as he was: mute, his head shaven, swaying back and forth to the sounds of suffering.

One day, for a reason unknown to me, he awoke from his silent dream. He ran towards me with tears streaming down his face. His eyes, which until then had been faraway, were piercing, manic.

'My name is Shmuel,' he cried. 'I am nine years old and my time has come. Promise me that you will say *kaddish* for me. Remember this day, this date. Remember my name. My name is Shmuel!'

I felt a cold wave of panic pass through my spine. I did not know what date it was, nor the day. I would forget Shmuel, his memory, his suffering, his eyes, his life, lost and anonymous among the bodies piled in that room by the hospital.

I looked down and saw the numbers tattooed on my arm: A27201. The number transfixed me, startled me with the starkness of its sudden permanence. 'A27201,' I said. 'This will be your *kaddish*.'

Shmuel was content, relieved that his God and his people would not forget him. He walked towards the exit of the barracks.

A27201 stays with me on my arm, and each time I look at it I'm reminded of Shmuel and all the other innocent victims who whispered *kaddish* with their final breath.

*

In spite of the horror around us, we were desperate to live. I used to look up at the stars every night, searching for guidance from my parents. It gave me hope.

A pregnant woman in our barracks gave Marta and me a teaspoon of her extra sugar rations each day, and we calculated that we would live an extra month on this. We made similar calculations over a tablespoon of porridge, which the same kind lady gave us.

Another time, someone threw a cigarette over the fence from the men's camp. Marta took it and peddled it for bread. Having learnt the trick with my shoes, she ran away with the bread and peddled the cigarette again and again.

One day, we were called out for *tzel apel* earlier than usual. The snow was well past our ankles.

'A prisoner has gone missing,' the *Blockälteste* told us, 'and until she is found you will wait outside in the snow.'

So we stood, for three days and three nights.

The poor young girl was found. She was dragged in front of us. I didn't feel angry at her for making us suffer in the snow like that. Her pain was my pain, my pain was her pain. She was so thin, so scared. They hanged her in front of us, forcing us to watch her punishment. I looked up at heaven.

Then I looked at Marta. She was ashen-faced, stiff. I dragged her inside and laid her down. All her toenails had fallen off.

Hospital

Auschwitz-Birkenau, December 1944–January 1945

A few days later Dr Mengele took Marta away. I screamed and cried as she was led away from the barracks. I was powerless, alone. But she came back not long after.

'What happened?' I asked, taking hold of her hands.

'They gave me injections,' she said. 'I don't know what they were. But I can't sleep. I have stomach cramps, I'm in pain.'

Next, Mengele decided that it was my turn. It was snowing that day and I was taken to the hospital wearing oversized wooden clogs. I prayed to God the whole way. It was daytime, so I couldn't speak to my parents through the stars.

In the hospital, I was assigned to a narrow bunk that I was to share with a Greek girl. We couldn't communicate – this was intentional – so we lay opposite each other in silence, our legs touching. We saw things together that no one should ever have to.

We saw twins bled to death. Their blood was transfused into a young healthy girl, who was then made pregnant.

We saw a pregnant woman give birth in the middle of the night. She delivered the baby herself, in silence. She held the baby for a moment in her arms, then placed it on the bunk, cut the umbilical cord and ran away. In the morning, Dr Mengele found the bed empty but for the baby. He shouted in fury and sent out a search party. He picked up the infant, injected it with some fatal medicine and hurled it across the room.

We saw a young boy return from surgery with scars on his abdomen. He sat on his bed in silence, comatose. And then, without warning, his scars split open and his organs began spilling on the floor.

We saw things together that no human should ever see. And we watched in silence, never sharing a word.

*

One morning a warden walked into our room and called my number. It was my turn to go.

I looked at the Greek girl. She looked back, and as I was dragged down from my bed she said, '*Shalom*.' She meant it as a goodbye, good luck, everything she could not express.

Soon inmates were holding me down, and standing in front of me was Dr Mengele. 'Extend your left arm,' he ordered. I struggled with the inmates, believing that they were going to kill me. It took a number of people to hold me down. I succumbed. Mengele came towards me with a needle and stuck it into my arm. I felt dizzy. I looked down and saw blood draining from my arm into a bottle. It came out thick and red. He filled four bottles with my blood, then withdrew the needle and walked away. I was forced back to my feet, weak and nauseous, and climbed back into bed with the Greek girl.

Over the next few days I was given a number of injections, just like Marta had been. We never found out what these injections contained. But since then both of us have suffered constantly from stomach cramps, and we have between us had several miscarriages. I was never allowed to breastfeed my own children.

*

In our barracks there was a mother and child. They were not Jewish so they were given special parcels from the Red Cross, which were filled with food, including sardines. They would eat the sardines and then throw the tails up to the ceiling, where they would stick. At night I would climb up the windowsills and peel the sardine tails off the ceiling. I have been mad about the taste of sardines ever since.

The non-Jewish child died a few days later. The mother wept for him. Because she was not Jewish, she was allowed to mourn her loss with a ceremony. His body was wrapped in

Hospital

coloured paper, prayers were said, and then he was cremated. I was jealous of the dignity with which he died.

*

One morning in the hospital we were woken up and given white bedclothes and new camp uniforms. Everything was cleaned and disinfected. I was confused. That afternoon, a delegation from the Red Cross walked into the barracks. They looked at us as if we were statues in a museum, detached, unemotional.

One woman in my ward, also named Eva, sat upright in her bed and shouted, 'This is an extermination camp! Our barracks have been made into a showpiece! Go and look at other barracks and at the gas chambers.'

'She is mad,' the SS officers accompanying the delegation said. 'Take her away.'

The Red Cross people simply ignored her. They did not ask any questions, not of her or any of us. That brave woman was publicly hanged the next day.

*

In the children's barracks we often talked about the Nazis losing the war, and our future. It helped us cope with the nightmare we were living.

We were petrified constantly. Any day could mean another experiment, or death. It was hell. Yet it was in that hospital that I made up my mind about my future. 'If I survive,' I told another child, 'I will have a large family and re-create everything that's being destroyed around us.'

We children would also talk incessantly about food and our families. We would dream up stories: everyone's parents were kings and queens, and everyone was rich and happy. We fantasised like this all the time. It helped us face the next torturous and fearful day.

Together we wrote a song of liberation, which we would sing, under our breaths, freezing, malnourished, during the dark nights. We would sing it to the tune of 'Hatikvah', the Zionist song that later became the Israeli national anthem.

Be happy and rejoice, handsome Jewish worker,
Soon this nightmare will end.
The great day of change is approaching
And the Jewish suffering will forever end.

We will return to our nice homes,
Embrace our beloved parents, whom we haven't held
*   for so long.*
There will be a table of plenty, beautiful clothes;
There will be toys, and nothing will ever go wrong.

The Sound of Defeat

Auschwitz-Birkenau, late January 1945

Around this time, bombs started dropping near the camp regularly. For us, it was the sound of liberation; for the SS, the sound of defeat. They must have known that defeat was inevitable, imminent. The tables of history had turned. But they would still not concede us our freedom, our survival. An evacuation commenced.

It was the middle of winter. We were lined up on the wide road that ran between the barracks, and for the last time we were forced to march for selection. The camp looked different. People were running and shouting. There was chaos.

A doctor stood in front of us. 'Those who are fit will be evacuated,' he explained. 'Those who are sick will stay behind.'

By this time, my body was weak with typhoid, dysentery and tuberculosis. I was undernourished and brutalised. I had nothing left. I walked past the SS man in charge of selection.

'You stay,' he ordered.

I had a sudden realisation that to stay would mean to die. Why would they leave us behind to live? Their evil had, so far, been inexhaustible. Why would it be different in defeat? They would wipe the sick out; they wouldn't let even one of us survive to tell our story. I was not going to capitulate now that freedom was in sight.

I joined the selection line again. This time, under the gaze of the SS man, I straightened my back and opened my eyes wide.

'You march,' he ordered.

*

To march meant to leave the camp and walk towards freedom. But as it turned out, I didn't have the strength even for that. I found Marta in the line and took her hand, and we walked back to the hospital. Amid the chaos, some other children joined us. We children, we were not choosing to stay or choosing to leave; we simply did not have the strength to choose.

The SS set fire to the hospital, and from there it spread. All of us who remained ran outside for safety, and we were caught between the burning buildings and the electric fences. Suddenly, there was a downpour, enough to put out the fires. For the first time the camp was quiet, morbidly so.

We had freedom, but it was a fearful freedom. We could do as we pleased, but the question remained: what should we do?

We were painfully hungry. Many made their way to the food chambers and started to eat, but I was too weak for that. Marta and I walked back to the barracks to sleep. The next morning we saw the bodies of those who had eaten themselves to death.

*

Three days later, to our horror, the SS returned. We were ordered to line up once again. This time there was no selection: march or be shot. We started to march. I held tight to Marta's hand. I was all she had, and she was all I had. When she faltered, I held her; when I faltered, she held me.

I was always together with Marta, step for step. When the SS men shouted, 'March!' we marched; when they shouted, 'Run!' we ran. People around us fell from exhaustion. They were shot. Marta and I kept going, always in the middle of the pack so that we could avoid the gaze of the SS men.

After several kilometres, we arrived at a different section of Auschwitz. We were rushed into a two-storey barracks. History unfolded in front of our eyes. The Russians, wearing white camouflage uniforms, fought hand to hand with the SS. Gunshots and grenades exploded all around us. It was all over quickly. The SS were outnumbered, overwhelmed, and they threw their hands up in surrender.

'You may come out now,' the Russian soldiers shouted. We emerged slowly from our barracks. Our tormentors were lined up, their hands still in the air, on a pile of snow. 'Do what you want with them,' the Russians said.

These men who had imprisoned us, beaten us, tortured us, killed our families, taken away our humanity, our hope – these men who had no mercy, even for children – were now trembling in the snow, begging for mercy. No one touched them. There was not even a whisper of revenge.

Was it that we were scared? Was it that we couldn't face death again? Perhaps. But, as we stood there in the snow, suddenly free, those men disappeared from our sight. What was left was an insatiable emptiness. A hunger, in body and soul.

The Russians walked among us, speechless. They did not look on us with sympathy, but with horror.

No One Was Waiting for Us

Auschwitz, 27 January 1945

After liberating Auschwitz, the Russians set up a hospital and ordered all the inmates to have medical examinations. The moment the Russian doctor laid eyes on me he sent me off to receive an immediate blood transfusion.

In the hospital they scrubbed my skin, seating me in a large bucket of water mixed with disinfectant, and then, to my horror, they shaved my head again. The hospital was overflowing. People were moaning and screaming in pain. Others died quietly, without protest.

I had dreamt of the day of our liberation; all of us children imagined that our parents would be waiting for us with toys and lollies. That vision had sustained us. Now, however, no one was waiting for us. No parents, grandparents, aunties or uncles; no lollies or toys. I was free, but I didn't feel free. I felt empty and confused.

Weeks passed in hospital; I have not much to say of them. Marta and I were empty vessels, weak, clinging to life. I remember that my skin was itchy with infections, and I would scratch at myself with filthy fingernails.

'We Are on Our Own'

Auschwitz, late March 1945

Sometime in early spring, I overheard some Russian soldiers making plans to take us children to Russia. Early the next morning, Marta and I crept out of the hospital. We scurried out of the gates of Auschwitz and into the soft spring air of the Polish countryside. The wind was gentle on my shaved head. I felt a sudden surge of freedom, of hope.

I looked back at the nightmare we had just survived. I saw the towers and the fences, and faces at the windows. They looked like thousands of skeletons, with their eyes all on me. 'Don't leave us,' they screamed.

Marta was trudging ahead in her oversized wooden clogs and camp uniform. I followed her, bearing the heavy burden of guilt at leaving those poor souls trapped in the nightmare.

We simply walked. We followed no direction, except away from Auschwitz, and the faster the better. We walked and walked. Night descended. We prayed together: *Please, God, lead us, help us, guide us. We are on our own and we don't know where we are.*

I lifted my eyes to the sky and looked at the stars. I had done this every night in the camps, remembering the last time I saw my Papa. Even in my darkest moments, the stars had kept me sane. They reminded me of my family, of warmth and protection. But on this night, lost in the Polish mountains, the stars were just stars. They were inert and uncaring, and they offered me no comfort. I felt that I had lost Papa. I was overcome by panic.

In the distance I saw a railway line. We walked towards it and began following the track. In the moonlight we could see a single carriage a little further down. We approached slowly: it was empty. Exhausted, we climbed inside, huddled together for warmth, then fell asleep.

In the middle of the night I woke up in a panic. At the opening of the carriage were Russian soldiers with their rifles aimed straight at us. I was paralysed. One of the soldiers switched on his flashlight and they immediately recognised us as little girls. They dropped their rifles, smiled, spoke in soft voices, hugged us and fed us bread and sweets.

'What are you little girls doing here?' the commander asked.

'We are survivors of Auschwitz,' I replied. 'We are trying to find our way back to Bratislava, but we are lost.'

'Bratislava is far away,' he said. 'We'll take you as far as we can. Once we drop you off, you can hitchhike with other army trucks. They are all going east.' He led us to his army truck and lifted us in.

'And take this,' he said, handing me a precious bottle of vodka. 'This will help convince others to take you for the ride. But get your little sister to offer it. She is smaller than you and more likely to attract sympathy.'

We rode with the soldiers through the dark hours of the morning until the first pinks of dawn appeared in the sky. We came to a fork in the road, and they let us out.

'Good luck,' the soldiers shouted.

*

We were alone again, directionless, somewhere in the Polish mountains. We walked in silence, without stopping, until it was dark.

'Maybe we should find a tree to sleep under,' I suggested.

Marta pointed to a light in the distance. It looked like a farmhouse.

Some time later, we approached it gingerly and knocked on the door. A tall Polish farmer with thick forearms opened the door. With downcast eyes, I asked: 'Excuse me, sir, would we be able to stay in your stable tonight? We are making our way home and have nowhere else to go. And perhaps, if you would be so kind, something to eat.'

The farmer was a kind man. He brought us each a large

glass of fresh milk and a slice of homemade bread. He watched us as we devoured the food with great satisfaction, then he showed us to his stable.

That night I was restless, unable to sleep. In the darkness I heard Marta whisper my name.

'What is it, Marta?' I asked.

'I can't sleep,' she whispered. 'I'm afraid of the cows.'

'Me too,' I replied.

The moment daylight broke, Marta and I left the stable and continued our journey. Just beyond the farmhouse we could see a highway that wound through the mountains. We walked towards it.

On reaching the highway, we were approached by an army truck filled with Russian soldiers. 'Go on, Marta,' I said. 'Show them the vodka.'

She stepped up to the side of the road, holding the bottle of alcohol above her head. The truck stopped and we were hoisted aboard.

Marta held out the bottle as an offering but none of the soldiers dared take it. They stared at us with pity in their eyes. I imagine their hearts were broken to see children, two little girls, in such a state.

After a few hours the soldiers told us they were no longer heading in our direction. We hopped out and started walking again, through the winding mountain passes, flanked by huge pines. It wasn't long before we were once again utterly lost.

We didn't see other travellers or soldiers for many miles. It was just us and the pines, and the rhythm of our wooden clogs. Then, in the distance, we saw a figure pushing a white trolley.

I stopped walking and held Marta's arm, curious to learn who this person might be. As he came closer, we could see his figure: he was a short, plump man sporting a white cap and gown. The trolley he was pushing was filled with ice cream of all flavours.

'Good day, little girls,' he said cheerfully, looking us up and down.

We remained in a stunned silence.

'You look like you could do with some ice cream. What flavour would you like? Free of charge.'

Marta and I looked at each other in disbelief. After months in the camps, with no more than watery coffee and stale bread, the prospect of ice cream was difficult to grasp. We were both so thirsty, craving fat and sugar. But an understanding from another time in our lives also passed between us. It was as if we could both hear Papa saying, 'Do not eat ice cream. It's bad for your health.' Papa's voice resonated with authority. It had so often been a guide for me in the past months. I could not disobey him now.

We declined the ice cream man's offer, and we continued in opposite directions.

Days of Walking

Somewhere in Poland, Spring 1945

Days of hitchhiking passed in a haze. Eventually, Marta and I found ourselves in Warsaw. The streets were filled with survivors, all looking for their families. They were skinny like us, empty like us. We were told that survivors were being processed at the Russian headquarters for refugees.

We were excited, deliriously happy. We thought that we had come to the end of our journey. All we had to do was register at the headquarters, we guessed, and then we would be sent home to our family. Marta and I talked impatiently as we walked to the office.

On the way I saw a familiar face. It was Mr Kohn, a family friend from Bratislava. The last time I had seen him was with his whole family on the cattle train from Sered' to Auschwitz. Now he was emaciated, his eyes sunken. Only he and his wife had survived; all their children were gone.

I didn't know Mr Kohn well, but still I was elated to see him. Seeing anyone we knew who had survived seemed like a miracle.

'Where are you going, Eva?' he asked.

'To the headquarters for refugees.'

He took me by the shoulders. 'For heaven's sake, don't go there! Do you know where they send orphans? They'll send you to Russia. No, Eva. You must continue your journey by foot. Get out of Warsaw before it's too late.'

Marta and I listened to Mr Kohn, and that evening we searched Warsaw for a safe place to sleep. The city was in a state of disrepair. We found a goods wagon filled with people. We could tell by their uniforms that they were survivors.

We climbed in. The survivors sat huddled on the floor like piles of rags, leaning against each other, almost weightless. Marta and I found a little corner to sleep in. I took off my clogs to rest my feet and fell asleep almost immediately.

In the morning I woke up and reached for my clogs. When I put on my left clog, I realised that someone – probably the old man sitting next to me, I thought – had relieved himself into it the night before. My foot was covered, and I let out a shout, horrified and sick.

All the survivors started to yell at me: 'You're disgusting! Why would you do that to your shoe?' Only the old man sat in silence, listening to the accusations.

Suddenly, the only thing that mattered to me was to rid myself of filth. My own clothes, my own skin became an unbearable burden. I had to be cleansed, to cleanse myself and wash away everything that had happened. For the next week I thought only of being clean.

*

Another week of walking, hitchhiking and begging for food passed by. I have not much to say of this time. My mind and my soul were elsewhere. My legs carried me. We eventually arrived in a town on the border between Poland and Slovakia. I turned to Marta. 'Let's find somewhere to wash,' I said. 'I need somewhere to wash.'

And then we heard the crack of gunshot and screams blaring from down the street. Survivors, still in their uniforms, were running. We heard cries: 'Pogrom!'

I became dizzy and leant on a streetlight, about to faint. At that moment I experienced the depths of despair. I felt that hatred, violence and killing was going to follow me through my entire life. There was no escape. I was doomed to run from it forever.

Suddenly, an army truck pulled up alongside Marta and me. It was a brigade of Jewish soldiers. They carried us into the truck and drove away.

Anywhere but Here

Poprad, Slovakia, Spring 1945

Eventually, we arrived in Poprad, Slovakia. Exactly how or when, I can't remember. I was disoriented. I was weak. I wanted so much to be at home with my parents, yet I still didn't know if they were alive. My memory of this time in my life is distorted by an intense anxiety.

In Poprad there was an 'absorption centre'. Marta and I were the only unattached children there among a throng of families and adult survivors. They did not help us. They were concerned with rebuilding their own lives, finding their own loved ones, and making their own way home. No one had time to help two little girls looking for their family. Everyone was looking for someone. Everyone was suffering.

The absorption centre gave out money to survivors for rations: one hundred crowns per week. I lined up with the adults and the money was placed directly in my hand. Never before had I been responsible for so much money.

Marta and I walked outside and showed each other our fortunes. 'We're rich!' we shouted. 'We can do whatever we want!' We hugged and danced in the street.

During our long walks through the Polish mountains, Marta and I had talked little, though when we did, it was about food. Particularly, we craved eggs. Now, we decided instantly: eggs, that was what we wanted.

We walked hand in hand to the grocer.

'How much are eggs?' I inquired, clutching my hundred crowns.

'Ten crowns for one egg.'

'I'll have ten eggs, please,' I responded happily, handing over my week's fortune. Marta also bought ten eggs.

We rushed back to the absorption centre and found a pot and stove to boil our loot. We put all twenty eggs in the boiling water, grinning from ear to ear as we did. Immediate satisfaction, delicious eggs.

After some minutes we pulled the eggs from the water and peeled them quickly, scalding our thin little hands. And we sat, Marta and I, cross-legged on the floor, in perfect silence and ate egg after egg, without pause.

The first few eggs were the perfect delicacy: creamy and nourishing. But as I put the eighth in my mouth, I began to feel sick. I had no choice but to finish them. I had seen people ready to kill for an extra crust of bread. I myself had been beaten when trying to feed milk to hungry infants.

With great discomfort, Marta and I devoured the last of our eggs. It was not a pleasurable experience. It was as if we had lost the capacity to enjoy ourselves.

*

It took us a few days to recover. Once we had digested the eggs, we were again overcome by hunger. But we had spent all of our money. We set off for a walk to the neighbouring village in search of food. We knocked on the doors of farmhouses and begged for bread. The farmers were, for the most part, generous. They gave us bread and milk.

We also went knocking on the doors of the apartments in the city, trying our luck. People in the city were absorbed in their own affairs. They gave us little time, and even less food.

One afternoon, all but overcome by exhaustion, Marta and I were walking along the avenue on which Poprad's most elegant apartments stood. I looked at the buildings enviously – no, not enviously, but bitterly. I remembered Palisády Ulica, how comfortable our life there had been.

Marta approached the front door of one of the apartments and knocked. The door opened. 'How can I help you?' a young man asked coldly. He was tall and blond, and he looked very familiar.

I peered inside and saw three other young people – another young man with blondish hair and two pretty girls – sitting around a table and playing cards. On the table stood a bowl of fruit and a bowl of chocolates. My mouth watered uncontrollably. Chocolate and fruit!

I looked back at the young man standing in the doorway. Yes, he was very familiar. I could tell by the way he looked at me that he recognised me too.

'Do I know you?' he asked.

The sound of his voice immediately took me back to the place where I first met him. He was one of the Rotstein boys who had asked my parents and me to hide his girlfriend in Klariská Ulica. They had survived.

'Yes!' I exclaimed. 'I am Eva Weiss. My parents hid your girlfriend, Judith, and your cousin in Klariská. They will remember me!'

I walked happily inside the apartment. I was ecstatic to be surrounded at last by people I knew. I also hoped they might be able to tell me something about my parents. But their eyes fell on me not with familiarity or gratitude – I had been the one to carry their excrement down to the sewer at Klariská – but with a meanness that I could not comprehend. Something in them had changed.

We talked briefly. I was distracted by the chocolates and fruit. I could smell the sweetness. But the Rotsteins did not offer us anything. The conversation was cold. It was as if they had forgotten that my parents had, without hesitation, taken in Judith and their cousin, saving their lives. The Rotstein boys would not even lend us a little bit of money for food. I asked for a loan and promised to repay them, but we left empty-handed, and broken-hearted.

Marta and I walked silently along the street, hungry, alone, rejected. Suddenly, we heard someone running up behind us.

'Eva! Wait!'

I turned around and saw Judith chasing after us. She had understood how hurt we were by their initial rejection.

'Eva,' she said, 'we can't lend you any money. I'm sorry. But we can help. Maybe one of you can come and stay with us. You will be safe. We have food to eat.'

'One of us?' I asked.

'It's a small apartment,' she explained. 'We don't have much space. We can't take both of you. I'm sorry, there just isn't room. You must understand.'

I felt angry and betrayed, but I knew that this was a good opportunity.

'Of course,' I said. 'Take Marta with you. And look after her.'

Without another word, Judith took Marta's hand and started walking back to the apartment, back to the chocolates and the fruit. I continued in the opposite direction, alone.

*

I was put under the care of a woman, Mrs Frankl, by the Jewish Joint Distribution Committee. She was loveless. Her entire family had perished, including her little sister, who would have been exactly my age had she survived.

From the moment I arrived, Mrs Frankl put me to work. She was not an adoptive mother; she simply used me as a servant. She didn't even give me a change of clothes. I was bound in servitude, stuck – fragile and weak – in the garments of my imprisonment.

I asked Mrs Frankl if she knew what had happened to my parents.

'They have been shot in Bratislava,' she said bluntly. 'You have no one left. You might as well give me your parents' bank details.'

I didn't believe her. I knew she just wanted my parents' money.

That afternoon I visited the Rotsteins' apartment and arranged with Marta that we would run away. 'I'll meet you tonight on the main highway, where the army trucks pass by,' I whispered in her ear. We had to continue our journey home.

That night was moonless. I crept out of Mrs Frankl's window and walked away without a word. Marta was waiting for me at the highway. We stood there together, without any belongings and without any sense of direction.

Anywhere but here, I thought to myself.

Convalescence

Tatra Mountains, Spring 1945

Marta and I hitchhiked in army trucks across the Slovak countryside, passing through little towns and farmland. There were displaced people everywhere, and utter devastation.

We eventually arrived in a large town that had another absorption centre for refugees. Unusually, it was orderly and clean. We registered and were then taken to the hospital for a medical examination.

A kind doctor took my pulse and held his hand over my chest. 'Breathe in . . . now breathe out.' I felt a familiar rasp in my lungs. I heard Marta's laboured breathing beside me.

'You both have tuberculosis,' the doctor said. 'We are sending you to the Tatra Mountains to recuperate.'

We were taken there in trucks. When we arrived, the mountains were just as I remembered from childhood: the sun shone, the air was clear, we had food to eat. But there was one thing missing that gnawed at my heart and my mind.

In the past, the Tatra Mountains had been a place of family. I thought back to our summer holidays: Papa arriving late from Switzerland with exotic fruits, *shabbos* with warm summer air coming through the windows. These were memories from a recent past – it was only a few years ago – but they felt like they were from someone else's life, not mine. Someone who was happy, without worry.

The girl in my memories wasn't me. She didn't have to worry about whether she would ever see her parents again, and which of her siblings was still alive. I was now someone else. Would that past life ever reunite with the one I was living now, or would the two remain forever separate?

I had no peace. I was regaining some of my physical strength, but mentally I was lost. I felt hopelessly isolated. I fantasised about running away from the hospital and making my way to Bratislava. But I was immobilised by fear.

They Are Alive

Tatra Mountains, May 1945

One afternoon, a few weeks after we arrived at the Tatra Mountains, a warm wind was blowing through the infirmary window. I was lying in bed next to Marta but was alone in my own head. We'd had no visitors; I didn't think anybody knew that we were there. We were alone.

Thoughts were swirling around in my head: *What if Frankl was right? What if my parents are dead and Marta and I are the only ones left alive? Where will we go? What will we do? How will we live?*

I heard the door to the infirmary open. I looked up and saw Mr Kohn walking towards us, smiling. The last time we had seen him was in Warsaw. He walked up to our beds, gave us both a hug and started talking.

I was confused. I looked at Marta and she looked back at me.

'I have good news for you,' Mr Kohn said. 'Bratislava has been liberated and your parents are alive.'

Marta and I immediately jumped out of our beds.

'Papa and Mutti?' I shouted. 'Are they really alive?'

'Yes, and they have sent me to bring you home. Now, lie back down for a moment. I need to explain a number of things.'

Mr Kohn told us that when Bratislava was liberated, the Jewish Joint posted lists of registered Jewish survivors all over the city. Papa and Mutti came out of hiding and immediately went to look for our names; they saw that we were staying in the hospital in the Tatra Mountains. By coincidence, Mr Kohn met Papa in the street soon afterwards. He told Papa that he had seen us in Warsaw and saved us from deportation to Russia. Papa, who was trying desperately to locate Kurti and my sisters, asked Mr Kohn to come and get us.

'I have to go now,' Mr Kohn told us.

'We'll come with you!' I shouted.

'No, you can't. I'm not your father, so you'll have to creep out of the hospital at night. Meet me out the front, and from there we'll hitchhike.'

For the rest of that day I was literally shaking with anticipation. That evening, we changed back into our camp uniforms under the sheets. When the hospital was quiet I tapped Marta on the shoulder and we crept out the front door.

Together with Mr Kohn, we walked in silence to the highway.

They Are Alive

*

The road was lined with refugees in their ragged clothes. Everyone was trying to get home, to find their families. Every now and then an army truck would slow; a throng of people would run towards it and throw themselves on.

It was hard for Marta and me to keep up with Mr Kohn. Everyone was running and pushing. I held tight to Marta's hand and we weaved our way through the crowd, following Mr Kohn's boots.

Suddenly, I lost sight of him. I looked around frantically, panicking. I heard someone shout through the crowd: 'Eva! I'm here. Hurry up!'

I looked up and saw Mr Kohn standing on the back of a truck, his arm stretched out to help pull us up. We sprinted towards the truck, pushed on all sides by others trying to get there. The truck rumbled and let out exhaust. It started moving further and further away. I looked at Mr Kohn's outstretched arm hopelessly.

'I'm so sorry,' Mr Kohn called out. 'You'll have to make it alone.'

I was furious. If Papa had come, this never would have happened. He would've waited for us. It didn't take long, though, for my anger to turn itself into resolve. I now had a purpose: get home to Mutti and Papa. They were alive! That was all that counted.

I can't tell you how many days it took for Marta and I to get home. We might've stood by that highway for many days before we were picked up, or it might've been just a few more hours. It didn't really matter.

All that mattered was that we found our way to a train station, and onto a train that would take us to Bratislava, to Mutti and Papa.

Arriving Home

Bratislava, June 1945

We got off at the Štefánikova Ulica train station. The last time I had been in Bratislava was when Papa had farewelled us. His words rang in my ears: '*Meine Kinder*, this might be our last goodbye . . .'

We walked briskly towards Palisády Ulica. Images of my childhood played out in my head. *Shabbat* meals of hot *cholent* and crusty *challot* that Mutti baked, the carp fished out of the bathtub, Mutti washing my hair in the basin, Papa rushing downstairs to say *kiddush* for his parents before returning to us. I was lost in my memories.

'Eva, look!' Marta said, bringing me out my reverie.

I raised my eyes and saw that we were approaching Palisády 60. I stood transfixed, staring at Papa and Kurti. They were standing outside the front gate of the building, talking to each other. They were dressed in their *shabbat* clothes, and looked thin yet dignified.

Neither of them moved, and nor did we. I was afraid. Perhaps this was just an illusion, one of my memories playing out before my eyes?

I looked carefully at Kurti. I hadn't seen him for years. He was so much taller, over six feet, and lanky. But his eyes were the same. They looked on me with love and care, and they offered protection.

Marta and I started to run towards Papa and Kurti. The four of us embraced, and I started to cry. Papa, in shock, put his hands over our heads and recited:

May God make you like Sarah, Rebecca, Rachel and Leah.
May God bless you and protect you.
May God's face shine toward you and show you favour.
May God look favourably upon you and grant you peace.

Kurti responded, 'Amen,' and opened the large wooden door to our house. I was overcome by a sense of familiarity. Perhaps it was the smell? And then I saw Mutti, standing just a few metres away. My beautiful mother was wearing an apron and a scarf, her face pale and her eyes sunken in dark shadow.

She was motionless. She did not say a word. We stayed by the door, not wanting to move until she did. I was frightened by her eyes, which had widened in horror. She was looking at me like I was a ghost. *Perhaps I'm too ugly for her now?* I thought to myself. *Perhaps she doesn't love me anymore? Perhaps she is ashamed to look at me?*

Slowly, Mutti inched towards us. She took Marta in one hand and me in the other. She led us through the house to the kitchen. It was filled with other children – not my siblings, but children just like me, sick and thin. They were orphans. Mutti was looking after them. In the middle of the room there was a small table with a large jam tin and bread on it. The children could help themselves.

Still without saying a word, our mother led us past the kitchen, through the back hallway and into a room. I saw a small white crib. Mutti took us over to it and rearranged the blankets. There, lying in sleep, was my little sister Rosanna. I had never met her. I didn't even know that she existed.

I later learned that Mutti had gone into labour while hiding in a garage in Bratislava. Papa was in hiding elsewhere, and Mutti had been forced to walk into the streets of Bratislava alone. She had approached a German soldier, and in her best Austrian accent said, 'Take me to a hospital.'

Mutti looked at Rosanna with great tenderness, and then, for the first time, looked down at Marta and me – really looked at us. At that moment her eyes became soft again, no longer horrified, and she knelt and hugged us both.

She arranged for us to be washed and clothed. I submitted myself completely to being cleaned and looked after. We were now living on the mezzanine floor of Palisády 60, where Pres Opapa and Pres Omama used to live. Soldiers from the Russian army were residing on the other floors.

We had *shabbat* dinner that first night we arrived home. Papa made *kiddush* on the wine and *ha'motzi* on the *challah*. Kurti stood next to him. The smell of *cholent* was heavy and overwhelming. I ate ravenously, greedily, unused to the idea of being able to keep eating. I made myself sick.

Everyone Returning

Palisády Ulica, Bratislava, Summer 1945

By the time Marta and I had arrived home, Kurti, Noemi, Ruth and Renata were also back at Palisády 60. They each had a story of survival that was filled with courage, despair, darkness, hope, perseverance and luck. But in those early days, as we were all returning to Bratislava, back into the warmth of my parents' care, we didn't talk about what had happened to us.

I later learned that Kurti and Noemi had survived while hiding in Bratislava. They were isolated completely from the outside world for a long time, and had to go for months without knowing whether any of their family was still alive. When Papa and Mutti went to retrieve them after the liberation of Bratislava, they were both skinny and weak from years of malnourishment.

Ruth and Renata, who had been hiding with Count Esterházy's coachman during the war, had been better looked after. However, after the German surrender, when the coachman refused to give them back to my parents, Papa had to pay a brigade of Russian soldiers to scour the outskirts of Újlak to find them. After a few weeks, the coachman was found and Ruth and Renata were brought back to Palisády Ulica.

Because Ruth and Renata were so young during the wartime years, they had forgotten about their lives beforehand. They did not remember anything of their Jewish lives. The first night Mutti put Ruth to bed, she had cried out, 'Where is my cross?' Her adopted parents had placed a crucifix opposite her bed.

One afternoon, Mutti took Ruth shopping. In the middle of the street Ruth let go of Mutti's hand and ran into a church across the road. Mutti followed and saw her daughter crossing herself with the holy water. Mutti pulled her out of the church.

'Ruth, you are Jewish,' she said. 'Do you understand?'

'I don't like your priests!' she shouted.

Not long after the end of the war, Mutti gave birth to my youngest sister, Hannah. Once again, Palisády Ulica was filled with young children. Our *shabbat* table was full, and when Mutti lit the candles I would sometimes be filled with the memory of an old tranquillity. I loved the two little ones, Rosanna and Hannah. I was very protective of them. I would take them for walks in the pram around Bratislava, and I'd make them call me 'Mummy'.

I was again surrounded by my siblings. It was a miracle that so many of us had survived. It was a miracle that my parents decided to continue having children. But things had changed. Our sweet little Judith had not returned to our family. Nor had any members of my father's family, whom he loved as much as his own. Their absence was a heavy silence that hung over us. They live on in the shared memory of my siblings and me.

I remain very close to my sisters to this day. We draw on each other for support. There is an understanding between us that cannot be articulated with words. Yet each of us has her own memory of this time in our lives, shaped by the passage of time and her personal experience of trauma.

Kurti

Palisády Ulica, Bratislava, July–August 1945

Days passed at Palisády 60. I started to regain some physical strength but my memories were a constant source of agony. I felt as if there was a deep layer of dirt that had infused my body. I spent days literally scraping my skin raw trying to get the dirt off. Kurti watched me with bewilderment and sympathy. By now he was fifteen and very mature, grown up. He did things with the self-assured calmness of a natural leader.

Kurti could speak fluent Hebrew and was learned in Jewish texts. He was also an avid Zionist. He was appointed head of the Bnei Akiva youth movement. Every *shabbat* Kurti would organise a meeting in the hills around Bratislava. He always insisted that I come. 'Eva,' he would say, 'this is a place where we can talk about Israel and *hachshara* with people our age. You must come.'

I often did go along. Kurti would stand in front of us and give a *sichah*, and he would talk about the future of the Jewish people in Israel. Many of us among the group were child survivors. We would latch on to Kurti's words: he spoke with such dignity and composure, while we still felt like wounded animals. I watched him and felt proud that he was my brother.

One Friday afternoon Kurti walked into my room. 'Eva, this *shabbat* you are going to give the *sichah* to the group.'

Before I had the opportunity to say no, Kurti began outlining what I should say and how I should say it. I listened, partly in admiration but also in bewilderment. I watched him pace around my room, tall and strong, his arms clasped behind his back. Every now and then he would pause. 'Eva, did you get that?'

I would shake my head.

'Very well. Then we start again.'

Kurti was infinitely patient with me in those early days of my recovery. He watched over me with kindness and concern.

One week a delegation of Israelis arrived in Bratislava. Kurti was the only one of us fluent in Hebrew, so he was assigned the task of welcoming them and showing them around the Jewish community.

Among the delegation were many young Israelis. They were all strong and dark, and carried themselves with vivacity. I remember how they looked at me. I saw in their eyes a similar look to Mutti's on the day Marta and I had arrived home. They tried to understand us, to comprehend what had happened to us. But it was impossible. Besides, no one had the courage, the strength to talk about what had happened.

*

Once again, my health started to deteriorate. I coughed throughout the night and was hopelessly lethargic. Marta was the same.

Mutti took us to the doctor. Our X-rays confirmed the doctor's diagnosis: tuberculosis. 'Mrs Weiss, TB is a contagious disease,' the doctor said. 'You have a young baby in the house. You'll have to send the girls away for treatment elsewhere.'

Mutti and Papa arranged for Marta and me to go to a rehabilitation centre in the Tatra Mountains. I was desperate not to leave them, and not to leave Kurti. I had also become very close to my sister Noemi. We had been close before the war, and now we were like soulmates; we understood each other without ever having to talk about it directly.

Papa and Mutti understood that I was distressed at the idea of being separated from the family once again. The morning we were to leave, they spoke to me plainly. 'Eva, you are sick,' they said. 'You can't get better here. But in the mountains you'll get well, and then you'll return and all of us will be together forever.'

I obeyed and asked no questions. Marta and I were taken by taxi to the Tatra Mountains in July 1945. The hospital was situated in a beautiful clearing in the mountains. Marta and I slept in fresh sheets, we had good food as often as we liked, and the fresh summer air blew in through the windows.

The doctors were kind and gentle. We were given injections of calcium-sandoz every day, and I felt strength returning to my lungs and my body. Nevertheless, at night I couldn't sleep.

*

It was Tisha B'Av two days after we arrived at the Tatra Mountains. Miles away, in Bratislava, Kurti recited *Eicha*, the Book of Lamentations. Papa later told me that his recitation held a heartbreaking symbolism.

O how has the city that was once so populous remained lonely? Just as in the past, the Jews of Europe were lamenting the destruction of the centre of their religious life. How was one to be Jewish after the Holocaust?

In my mind's eye I can picture Kurti standing before the decimated community of Bratislava's Jews, his young voice echoing the lamentations of his people's history, their suffering. But I was miles away, lying in bed, awake.

She weeps, yea, she weeps in the night, and her tears are on her cheek; she has no comforter among all her lovers; all her friends have betrayed her; they have become her enemies.

Two days after Tisha B'Av, the members of Bnei Akiva planned to make a trip outside Bratislava, to the Danube.

'Mutti,' Kurti said at the dinner table, 'I have an excursion tomorrow with Bnei Akiva. My bathers need mending. Would you be able to help me?'

Papa, who usually supported Kurti's work at Bnei Akiva, stood up and slammed his fist into the table. 'I strictly forbid you from going!' he shouted, and left the room.

Mutti understood that Papa's reaction was just protectiveness. She winked at Kurti and the matter was closed: he could go.

Early the following morning, Kurti left the house without saying goodbye to Papa. Papa heard the gate close. He quickly jumped out of bed and ran into the street, but Kurti had already disappeared with his friends.

That whole day an uncomfortable feeling followed Papa – a premonition, perhaps. In the early afternoon he misplaced a briefcase containing a hundred thousand crowns. Papa, usually a fastidious man, was perplexed. He didn't want to find it because he considered it a bad omen. God could keep the briefcase in payment for Kurti's safe return, he decided.

Not long after, Papa found the briefcase sitting in the middle of his study. He was deeply troubled by this. He opened the briefcase, took out the money and asked Mutti to stuff it into a cushion. There was something wrong that day: Papa could feel it. He could not distract himself from his own thoughts, his anxieties.

The sun sank and the summer sky turned purple. Kurti had not returned. It grew darker, and then the sky was black; it was a moonless night. Still, Kurti had not returned.

Overcome by panic, Papa began walking the streets in search of his only son. He ran to the houses of every other leader at Bnei Akiva and knocked on their doors. There was no response; they were hiding from him. He ran through the night, knocking on doors, screaming, 'Where is my Kurti?' But no one answered.

I was away when it happened, somewhere in the Tatra Mountains, probably lying awake. I was not there to see the look on Papa's face when he finally found out what had happened to his son. (I only found out years later, in Israel, when a young man who had been there that day – Anton Fischer, who lived in Melbourne – arranged to meet me.)

The kids on the excursion were swimming in the Danube. They saw a group of Russian soldiers approaching and decided to get out of the water. They ran into the forest and hid, fearing that the girls might be raped. At the same time, Kurti was caught in an undercurrent and began waving to them for help. The group had to choose between saving Kurti or running into hiding. They hid and Kurti was left to drown.

I wasn't there when Papa went looking for Kurti's body. Papa found his only son floating lifeless in the waters of the Danube. Nor was I there when his body was drawn out with horse and cart and taken back to Bratislava. The whole city mourned, but I could not mourn along with them. Mutti and Papa did not tell Marta and me. They feared it would be too much for us.

Eicha, the Book of Lamentations, begins with the word 'how'. How? How, after all that we had been through, could this happen?

The Lord has become like an enemy; He has destroyed Israel; He has destroyed all its palaces, laid in ruins its strongholds, and increased in the daughter of Judah pain and wailing.

Boarding School

BEX-LES-BAINS, SWITZERLAND, 1946–1948

It didn't take Mutti and Papa long to realise that life in Bratislava was impossible. There are certain wounds that cannot heal. They decided to send my sisters and me to a Jewish boarding school in the French-speaking region of Switzerland. It was called the Dr Ascher Institute in Bex-les-Bains.

I was relieved to get out of Bratislava, away from all those memories, and away from the anti-Semitism that persisted even after the war. I was fairly happy at boarding school because there were constant distractions. We learned to speak French, to socialise with others our age. We were taught how to ski and we developed a love of French poetry. My life there had order.

Monsieur Ascher was very strict. He made us jump into an unheated swimming pool to test our resolve, and if he caught us looking at our neighbour's plate during mealtimes, he would take away our food. He didn't understand the anxiety this caused in Marta and me; he didn't know what had happened to us. No one did.

Mutti and Papa would visit often and bring us delicacies: smoked turkey, roast duck, chocolates. Mutti also made sure to bring us new clothes. I remember when she bought me my first bra. I felt grown up and important.

In a way, I flourished in Switzerland. After two years I graduated with first-class honours, and I came second in my class for athletics and table tennis. But I still found night-time difficult. I couldn't help but feel that I was being held somewhere against my will, that I was institutionalised. I didn't share these fears with anyone.

*

After two years of relative peace, we returned to Bratislava. We discovered that Mutti and Papa had plans to take us to live in Australia.

'Why Australia?' I asked Papa one evening. 'Why not Israel?'

'It is the furthest place from here,' he said.

The Furthest Place from Here

BRATISLAVA, SLOVAKIA, 1948

Papa had to flee Bratislava before our papers to Australia had been formalised. The Soviets were closing the borders – putting up the Iron Curtain – and the KGB was arresting those whom they considered 'capitalist enemies'. Papa escaped by train to Switzerland, leaving Mutti and us girls behind.

From Switzerland, Papa arranged for Mutti to sell our house to the Hungarian Embassy for a reasonable price; in return, they would grant us visas to travel through Hungary to Switzerland. The Hungarians kept their promise, but my passport had almost expired and so they did not issue me a visa.

When we boarded the train from Bratislava to Budapest, I moved from the carriage Mutti and my sisters were in because Mutti was kissing Ruth over and over – it was driving me insane. Before the train left the station, however, I was approached by the border police, who asked to see my visa for Hungary. When they found that I did not have one, they took me off the train. I asked them if they would have allowed me to continue my journey if I did have a visa. Their answer was yes.

Then, on the other side of the platform, I saw Mutti and my sisters being taken off the train by the same border police. I ran across and told the border police that they themselves had just told me that anyone with a visa could travel to Budapest. They begrudgingly let Mutti and my sisters back on the train. I assured Mutti that I would be okay, that Papa would look after things.

Somehow, Papa discovered that I hadn't made it to Budapest with Mutti. I spoke to him on the phone.

'Eva, I'm sorry you've had to stay behind in Bratislava alone,' he said. 'Listen to me: go to the Hungarian Embassy. They're going to send you to the border of Austria and Switzerland with a team of professional swimmers. I'll meet you there.'

I did exactly as I was told. During the journey, I was interrogated and searched by Russian soldiers. They were looking to see if I was smuggling money from Slovakia into Austria. They confiscated my dearest possession, a book of Hebrew poetry Kurti had written and given me.

Eventually, we arrived at the Swiss border and I was greeted by Papa. He cried with relief, 'Eva!' We were both exhilarated. From there, we continued our journey to Lugano, where Papa had rented an apartment.

It was a sunny and mild day when Papa and I arrived. We walked up the stairs of our apartment building, and Papa opened the door.

There were my sisters playing, and Mutti standing by the window, looking out over the mountains. Warm light was bursting through the room. Mutti turned to me and smiled. For a moment, I felt safe, I felt happy.

*

But it was just a moment. Still no one spoke of the nightmare that we had all survived. Although reunited, we were still alone.

Most of our closest family members had perished, but we did not speak about it. We were silent. We did not speak of my grandparents, or of Uncle David and Auntie Frida, of Uncle Shamu and his wife and their children, my cousins. These people, who had been the foundation of our lives before the war, were now gone. All of them gone. We did not speak of the camps and hiding and torture, of starvation and cruelty and loneliness. We did not speak of Judith, our little Judith. My sister, my parents' daughter. No one said a word.

It was unspeakable at this stage. Unutterable. Too vivid. It was as if to mention it was to confirm that it was over – and perhaps it wasn't? And so my experiences and emotions played themselves out in my head at night. They tormented me and isolated me from my parents, even from Marta. We couldn't communicate, even though we had shared so much. Our tongues were bound in a shameful silence, heavy with some sort of guilt or remorse.

This weight has stayed with me my entire life. I was never able to talk to my parents, my darling Mutti and Papa, about what happened to me. They passed away, years later in Australia, without me ever having said a word. I couldn't bear to tell them, to show them how I suffered.

I didn't want them to know what had happened because I wanted them to be the same Mutti and Papa they had been before everything. I wanted them to look at me as their little, happy Eva, not as a survivor of Auschwitz. I didn't want them to know what I had seen.

But the silence resolved nothing; it only made things worse. Something had been broken that would never be repaired, I knew, even if we tried to talk about it.

This is the suffering we were all forced to carry alone for many years. It is the suffering of a last goodbye that happened at the train station many years ago. Papa had looked into my eyes: '*Meine Kinder*, this might be our last goodbye . . .'

It wasn't just a goodbye between father and daughter, I came to realise. It was the goodbye to a family, to a people, to a time in history. It was the final goodbye to an entire way of life.

Epilogue

It took us six weeks to travel by boat from Genoa to Australia. The journey aboard the SS *Napoli* was rough and we were all horribly seasick. There was no kosher food to eat except for boiled potatoes and occasionally a boiled egg.

The men and women were separated into crowded dormitories; we had to store our luggage under our small bunk beds. Mutti minded with great care a suitcase filled with our most precious belongings, which she had smuggled out of Bratislava – the items she and Papa had managed to hide under a concrete slab in the cellar at Palisády 60. The most precious among these possessions was the Weiss family *sefer Torah*.

The first place we lived after arriving in Melbourne was a small house at 153A Nicholson Street, East Brunswick. I remember that our neighbours were fabulous – so friendly, gentle and kind. It was difficult, though. I was seventeen and really wanted to be in Israel. That's where all my friends were. I resented that, and during our first few weeks in Australia I refused to learn English or the currency. But it didn't take long for me to accept my new environment.

It was harder for my parents, particularly Papa. He was quite depressed when we arrived. He didn't have the language; he wasn't the big businessman that he had been in Bratislava. My sisters and I had to protect him. He bought a wafer factory in East Brunswick – a business we had no idea about – and we all helped.

One thing that made Papa happy was going to the East Brunswick *shul* to pray on *shabbat*. Just a few days after we arrived, he introduced himself to the local rabbi and offered to lend our *sefer Torah* to his congregation. On *shabbat* mornings, a portion from our *sefer Torah* was always read aloud.

Eventually, we moved from East Brunswick to South Caulfield, and shortly after to Balaclava Road, East St Kilda, where the Jewish community was more vibrant and tight-knit. I married my husband, Ben Slonim, in 1953, and we lived on Inkerman Street in a small unit. Mutti and Papa lived just down the road, next to Mizrachi *shul*; they again lent our *sefer Torah* to the congregation to be read from on *shabbat*.

Our family grew. I had five children, and my sisters had children of their own. Years passed, and suddenly there were grandchildren everywhere, both in Australia and in Israel. I felt as if the ardent desire that had grown in me during my time at Auschwitz – to re-create what had been lost – was being fulfilled.

When Papa passed away in 1984 I helped Mutti organise his belongings. Inside a locked drawer in his desk were the

Epilogue

documents he had hidden from the Nazis under the concrete slab at Palisády 60. There were papers attesting to the fact that our business had been confiscated, and that Papa had been enlisted as forced labour. There were the notes that Auntie Frida had sent to Mutti and Papa from the camps, as well as the yellow stars we had once been forced to wear. There were also dozens of old photographs – pictures of Pres Opapa and Pres Omama, of my sweet cousins who hadn't survived, and of my little sister Judith, her hair in pigtails, at the train station in Bratislava – the last time I ever saw her.

These documents have since been copied and stored at the State Library of Victoria and at the Holocaust Museum in Melbourne. They provide concrete evidence of the truth of my oral testimony. More than that, though, for me they are the final link to a life we once lived.

Perhaps more than photos and documents ever could, it is the Weiss family *sefer Torah* that provides me with a sense of continuity. I have watched proudly as my children and grandchildren have read from it on their bar or bat mitzvahs. To listen to their voices as they recite the same passages that our ancestors once did, reading from the very same scroll that was once housed in Bratislava – this is a living memory. It is something from my past that is once again alive, flourishing.

Acknowledgements

I thank Australia, land of tranquillity and plenty, for granting my family refuge. I thank my whole family, both in Australia and Israel, for your constant love and support. I thank Nicole Gershov for helping me start down this path of memory. I thank Oscar Schwartz for guiding me through this journey. I thank my husband, Ben Slonim, for his unwavering support in all my endeavours.

Now that we, the last witnesses to the Holocaust, are approaching the end of our lives, I ask myself: is my survival a privilege, a reward, a punishment or a charging of great responsibility? It is all of those. I feel that it is my sacred obligation to be vigilant, to preach tolerance, to rebuild, to perpetuate and to commemorate the memory of the one and a half million children who vanished without graves and without tombstones.

Glossary

aliyah – to migrate to Israel

arizátor – non-Jews appointed to run confiscated Jewish businesses

Blockälteste – the inmate in charge of a concentration camp barracks

challah (pl. *challot*) – an egg loaf traditionally eaten during the Sabbath meal

cheder – place of learning

chevrah kadishah – the organisation appointed to oversee Jewish funerary rituals

cholent – a traditional Jewish dish of beans, meat and potatoes, eaten on the Sabbath

davening – praying

emet – truth

Familienlager – the family barracks

Gilgul – the concept of reincarnation in Kabbalah

ha'motzi – a prayer for bread

hachshara – programs in Israel, aimed at personal and ideological development

Glossary

Hausmeister – caretaker
Judenfrei – free of Jewish inhabitants
kaddish – the Jewish prayer for the dead
kapo – a prisoner in a concentration camp who was given the role of supervisor of other prisoners by the SS
kasher – the process by which meat becomes edible, according to Jewish law
kiddush – prayer for the wine on Sabbath eve
Kinderzimmer – children's room
kneidel – a dumpling, usually served in chicken soup
kollel – an institute for full-time advanced study of the rabbinic literature for married men
muktzeh – items and activities forbidden on the Sabbath
Nokkerln – small potato dumplings
payot – sidelocks
Pesach – Passover
Raus! – Out!
rosh kehilah – the head of a community
schishkelach – a meat stew
schpazier – a slow stroll
seder – the Passover meal
sefer Torah – a Torah scroll
seudah shlishit – the third meal during the Sabbath
shabbat, *shabbos* – the Jewish Sabbath
sheitl – a wig worn by a married Jewish woman
shochet – slaughterer

Glossary

shul – synagogue

sichah – a lesson

stubova – helper

tallit – prayer shawl worn in Synagogue by married Jewish men

Totenkopf – skull and crossbones

tzel apel – roll call

tzimmes – cooked carrots

tzitzit – fringes or tassels worn on traditional or ceremonial garments by Jewish males

Unnetaneh Tokef – a prayer said on Yom Kippur

vidui – a confessional prayer said on the Day of Atonement

yom tov – a blanket name for a holiday during the Jewish year

zikaron – memory